Motor Cruising Handbook

and

Practical Course Notes

Written by Simon Jinks

Illustrations by Sarah Selman

2004

For artistic purposes lifejackets are not shown being worn in the illustrations. The RYA strongly advises that lifejackets are worn at all times for watersports.

Foreword

The RYA Motor Cruising Handbook is designed to accompany RYA motor cruising courses, taught at RYA training centres around the world. It also provides a wealth of valuable information to all those thinking of going to sea.

More detailed information on specific subjects can be gained by reading:

RYA Day Skipper or Yachtmaster Shorebased Notes.

These books cover the theoretical side of navigation, seamanship, meteorology and collision avoidance (Rules of the Road). They support the RYA Day Skipper and Yachtmaster courses.

RYA Radar, RYA Electronic Navigation, RYA Weather Handbook, RYA Navigation Handbook, RYA Powerboat Handbook.

These books give detailed information on specific subjects and are designed to be used by all boaters.

Practical courses

There is no substitute for experience. No matter how detailed the book, practical experience on board a boat with a trained instructor is worth its weight in gold. For the best possible preparation, use this book in conjunction with RYA tuition.

RYA practical courses include:

RYA Helmsman Course
RYA Day Skipper Course
RYA Coastal Skipper Course

© 2004 RYA

First Published 2004
The Royal Yachting Association
RYA House Ensign Way Hamble
Southampton SO31 4YA
Tel: 0845 345 0400
Fax: 0845 345 0329
E-mail: info@rya.org.uk
Web: www.rya.org.uk

British Cataloguing in Publication Date:
A Catalogue record of this book is available from
the British Library.
ISBN:
Acknowledgements: UKHO, Paul Sumptner, C-Map UK LTD.
Photographic credits: Simon Jinks, Grand Banks, Deva Marine.

Design and production by: Avalon Design+Print
Cover design: Pete Galvin

Contents

Contents

Contents

Introduction

There are many different types of craft on the water and you'll probably try a few before settling for the one that suits you best. Some boats are built as tools for fishing, skiing or as workboats, others are built for comfort or speed. All of them, however, are the result of compromise, and it will be hard to find a boat that suits all your needs all the time.

Whichever boat you opt for and wherever you use it, its basic operation works on the principles set down in this book. Whether you are fishing or cruising the coast, the same pre-start checks will have to be done before leaving port, the same safety issues will need to be considered and the same manoeuvres will have to be performed to get to the open sea. We all travel on the same sea – it's just that our final destinations are different.

Although it would be impossible to include every imaginable scenario in this book, we hope to give you the knowledge to assess a situation correctly and make an informed decision on what to do next.

Safety, preparation and briefing are the most important points to consider when going to sea, and you must be well informed and well prepared before you leave harbour. And if in doubt during any manoeuvre or pilotage situation, slow down and give yourself time to think the situation through. Your aim is to think, at least, one step ahead all of the time, to try to anticipate what is going to happen next.

Types of motor cruiser

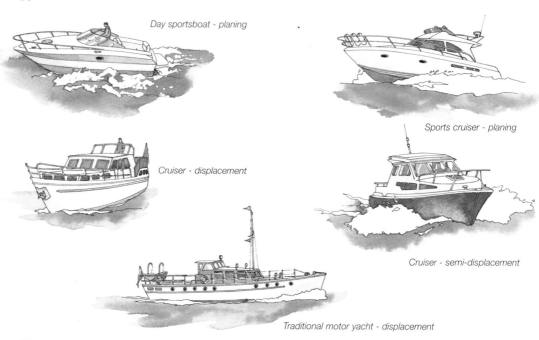

Day sportsboat - planing

Sports cruiser - planing

Cruiser - displacement

Cruiser - semi-displacement

Traditional motor yacht - displacement

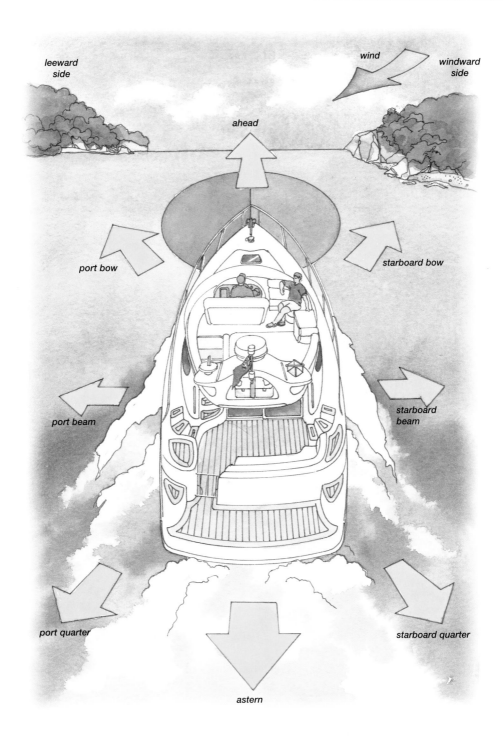

leeward side

wind

windward side

ahead

port bow

starboard bow

port beam

starboard beam

port quarter

starboard quarter

astern

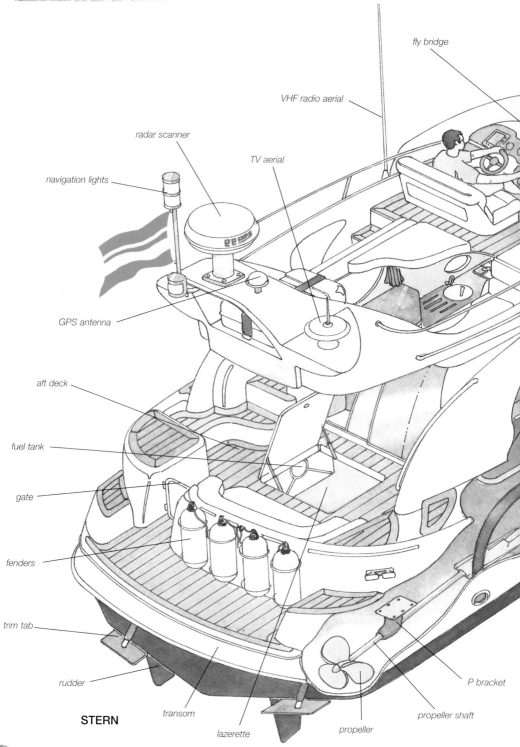

fly bridge

VHF radio aerial

radar scanner

TV aerial

navigation lights

GPS antenna

aft deck

fuel tank

gate

fenders

trim tab

rudder

P bracket

STERN

transom

propeller shaft

lazerette

propeller

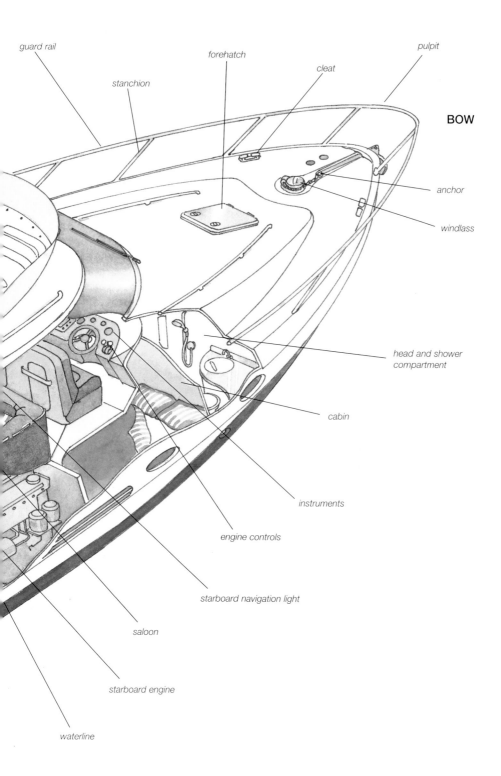

guard rail

forehatch

cleat

pulpit

stanchion

BOW

anchor

windlass

head and shower
compartment

cabin

instruments

engine controls

starboard navigation light

saloon

starboard engine

waterline

3 Safety kit

Safety brief checklist

- A good skipper should give a safety brief to new crew containing the following points.
- How to put on and use lifejackets.
- Flares – how they operate.
- Abandon ship procedure.
- Bilge pumps.
- Gas.
- First aid kit location.
- Heads – how they operate.
- Fire extinguishers.
- Man overboard procedure.
- Sending a Mayday or DSC alert.

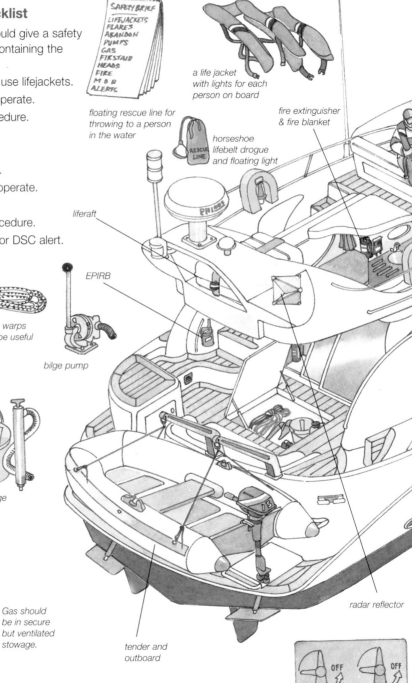

SAFETY BRIEF
LIFEJACKETS
FLARES
ABANDON
PUMPS
GAS
FIRST AID
HEADS
FIRE
M O B
ALERTS

a life jacket with lights for each person on board

floating rescue line for throwing to a person in the water

horseshoe lifebelt drogue and floating light

fire extinguisher & fire blanket

liferaft

EPIRB

extra warps can be useful

bilge pump

spare water and fuel

hand bilge pump

Gas should be in secure but ventilated stowage.

tender and outboard

radar reflector

fuel taps

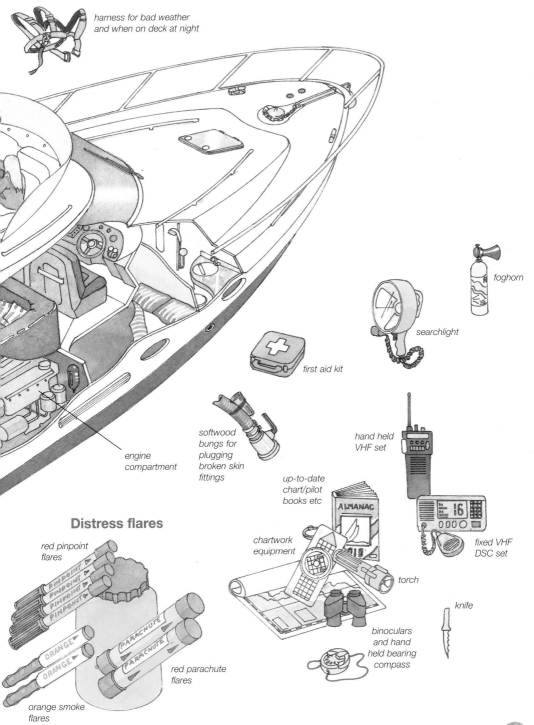

harness for bad weather
and when on deck at night

foghorn

searchlight

first aid kit

engine
compartment

softwood
bungs for
plugging
broken skin
fittings

hand held
VHF set

fixed VHF
DSC set

up-to-date
chart/pilot
books etc

ALMANAC

Distress flares

chartwork
equipment

torch

red pinpoint
flares

knife

binoculars
and hand
held bearing
compass

red parachute
flares

orange smoke
flares

4 Engine checks

There are no lay-bys or garages at sea – therefore an engine needs to be thoroughly maintained to ensure it does not break down. Because the sea is a very harsh environment, it requires daily checks. Consult the engine manual for the definitive list of checks on your make of engine.

Good practice

- Keep the engines clean and solve any leaks promptly. Use oil-absorbing pads to catch oil drips to prevent fluid spreading through the bilge and becoming a fire hazard.

- Condensation can occur in fuel tanks – keep them topped up to reduce this possibility.

- Pinch and flex rubber pipes to look for signs of perishing.

- Sacrificial anodes fitted on the shaft and in the engine block protect the engine from corrosion; ensure they are changed at manufacturer stated intervals.

- Have a quick look at the engine, before, during and after a passage this gives advance warning of potential problems.

Daily Checks

Fresh water: check coolant level

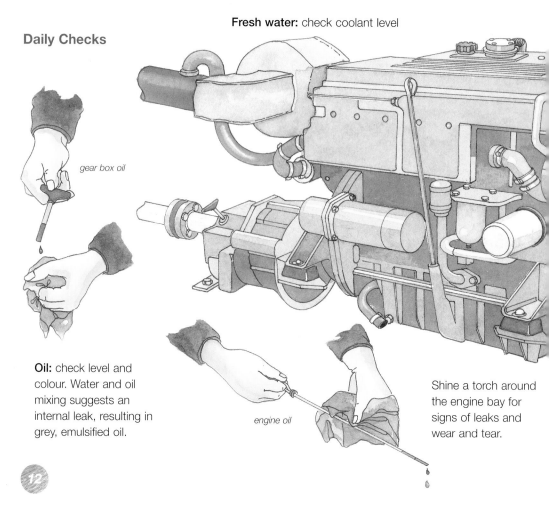

gear box oil

engine oil

Oil: check level and colour. Water and oil mixing suggests an internal leak, resulting in grey, emulsified oil.

Shine a torch around the engine bay for signs of leaks and wear and tear.

Engine seawater inlet and strainer: Check for debris in engine seawater inlet strainer. Remember to re-open seacock if shut during check.

seacock

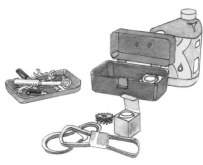

Carry spares

- Fuel filters.
- Belts.
- Water pump impeller.
- Oil.
- Tools.

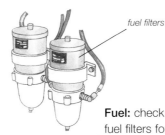

fuel filters

Fuel: check fuel level. Check fuel filters for signs of water or debris.

Belt tension: check tension of all belts: steering, alternator, and water pump.

Weekly or after 30 hours usage:

- Check gearbox oil level.
- Check hydraulic oil for outdrive and tabs.
- Adjust alternator/pump belt tensions if required.
- A visual check of engine hoses and hose fittings.

5 Control checks

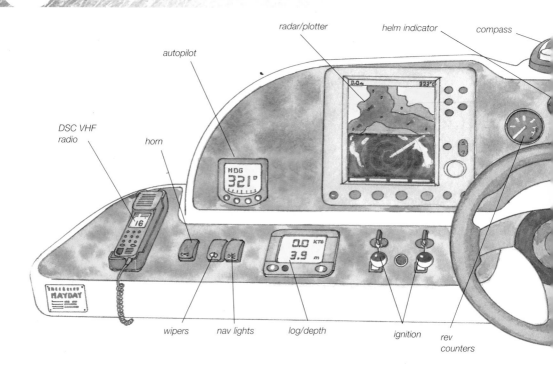

autopilot · radar/plotter · helm indicator · compass

DSC VHF radio · horn

wipers · nav lights · log/depth · ignition · rev counters

Engine-gauge information should be recorded in an engine logbook, or by marking the gauges themselves using a chinagraph pencil or correction fluid. Any small differences will then be detected throughout the year, helping fault diagnosis and troubleshooting. During a passage, the engine log may help you to deduce that one engine is running hotter than usual, or that more revs are required to do the same speed than on a previous occasion.

Water temperature – mark normal operating temperature.

Volts – check initial voltage rise to indicate charging.

Oil pressure – mark minimum and maximum (pressure changes with revs).

Revs/speed – the relationship between these two can let you know if there is weed growth on the hull or there is damage to the props.

Helm indicators – these indicate the position of the rudder. A boat's wheel does not self-straighten like a car, and it is easy to forget which direction the rudder is pointing during slow manoeuvring.

Throttle – these are controlled by cable or electronics. Electronic throttles are light to use but may have a time lag. Find out the amount of delay whilst alongside by briefly engaging the gear. Ensure the *Neutral* point is marked, so the engine is not accidentally left in gear.

Some installations utilise a changeover switch to change throttle priority between flybridge and cockpit steering positions.

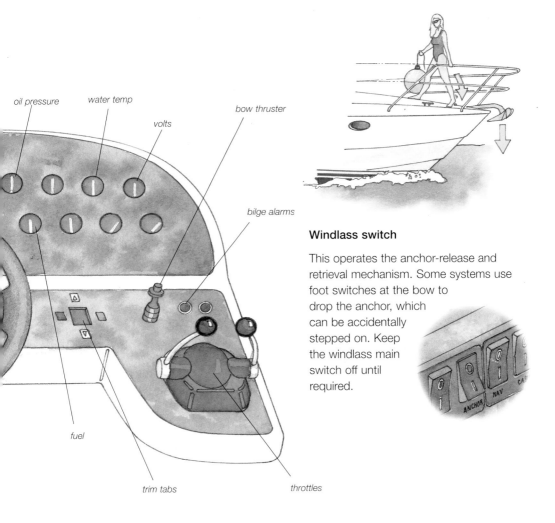

oil pressure water temp volts bow thruster

bilge alarms

fuel trim tabs throttles

Windlass switch

This operates the anchor-release and retrieval mechanism. Some systems use foot switches at the bow to drop the anchor, which can be accidentally stepped on. Keep the windlass main switch off until required.

Engine starting

Batteries – ensure batteries are switched to ON or ALL.

Set throttles – turbocharged engines should be started with the least revs possible. Non-turbo engines are usually set to half revs.

Preheat – initiate preheat on some diesel engines to help starting.

- Once the engine is started, reduce revs to a minimum rpm – do not over-rev before the oil has had time to circulate.

- if visible check that the cooling water is discharging normally through the exhaust outlet.

- Check gearshifts by gently easing into forward and astern for a few moments.

- Some engine start-up procedures are completely automated. Turn the key and the throttles pre-set and the engines start up after a preheat sequence.

- Diesel engines like working under load – do not stay in neutral for too long, and if possible get underway as soon as possible. Avoid maximum speed until the engines are up to operating temperature.

6 Before you go

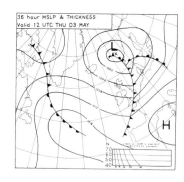

- Check the weather forecast.

- Switch radar to stand-by to reduce the chance of the scanner emitting electro-magnetic radiation.

- Last look around to check that the exit is clear.

- Remember to unplug shore power, pontoon end first.

- Rig slip lines and position fenders for leaving.

Brief the crew (see page 10)

Prepare a navigational plan and pay particular attention to the harbour exit and entry as well as speed bylaws. Brief the crew; making sure they are aware of their roles for departure. Ensure new crew are given a safety brief and told how to move around deck; 'one hand for the boat and one hand for yourself'.

Once underway and still in sheltered water, remove lines and fenders Move the crew back into a safe position before attaining cruising speed in open water. Be gentle on the throttle to ensure the crew are not thrown off their feet.

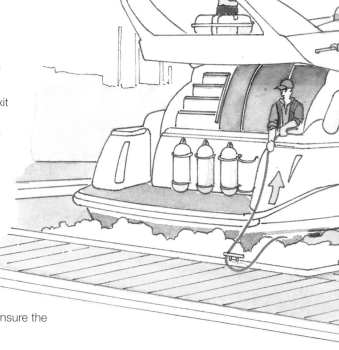

Wear protective clothing, and keep warm.

Prepare enough food and drink for the trip–
food preparation at sea can be difficult.

Stow all loose items.

Do not drink and drive.

Issue and fit lifejackets –
ensure the crew know how
they operate.

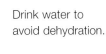

Drink water to
avoid dehydration.

Motorboat Industries
13265146217

"Seaswift 31"
CATAGORY B

Max 🧍 = 8
Max 🧍 + 📦 = 1000 kg
CE 0609

Do not overload –
see the vessels CE
plate and the
section on stability,
on page 118.

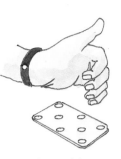

Use anti sea-sickness
remedies.

7 Propulsion & steering

Hull configuration and engine layout

Single screw (A single-screw arrangement)

A single propeller drives the boat and can be used in high-speed planing hulls or in displacement boats. The diagram shows a displacement boat, which would typically give low speed and low fuel consumption. Pulling power is typically good, as the size of engine will be chosen for torque rather than faster speed. They require good synchronization between rudder and throttle for effective control in close quarters.

Twin screw

This is by far the most common arrangement, engines inside the boat drive the propellers via shafts fitted outside. The engines can be placed nearly anywhere in the boat as long as the shafts are near the stern. Shafts are placed further away from the centreline, allowing greater turning action from each engine when used in close-quarter manoeuvres.

Outdrives:

Sometimes known as inboard/outboards. Outdrives feature engines inside the boat with the gearbox and propeller outside. They are fitted close to the centreline to ensure the props are in contact with the water when the hull rises onto the plane. The outdrive leg steers the boat and tilts to allow fore and aft trim.

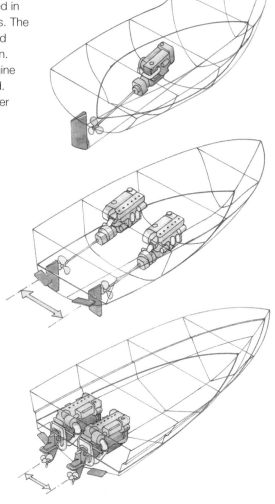

Water jet

Instead of the shaft turning the propeller, an engine-driven prop shaft turns an impeller. The impeller sucks water from underneath the boat through a grating and jets it out of the stern through a smaller hole, at higher pressure, propelling the boat forward. The jet is steered in a similar way to an outdrive leg, a bucket drops over the jet to reverse the jet of water, allowing the craft to go astern. Water-jet units are useful for shallow-water use, and where props could be a danger – such as rescue work or diving.

Planing

A planing hull rises onto its own bow wave, and then sits on top of the water rather than in the water. Friction of the hull against the water is greatly reduced, and as more power is added, speed increases. Common types of planing hull are deep or shallow vee and hard chine. Deeper vee sections cushion the impact in rougher weather, as they cut through the sea. If a planing craft has relatively flat underwater hull sections, it will slam against waves.

Stepped hulls are planing boats that have steps cut into their hull. The steps break the water flow passing over the hull allowing a cushion of air underneath the hull. This lowers friction further to the extent that very little of the boat is in the water so allowing a further increase in speed. Caution should be taken when cornering, and when used in moderate sea states as they are prone to flip or roll when one side of the hull digs in the water. The cushon of air can cause a loss of control.

Displacement

A hull that is sitting in water is displacing water and is said to be in displacement mode. As power and speed increase, a displacement hull will keep displacing water and simply push its way ahead; unlike a planing hull that rises up on its bow wave. Displacement craft are limited in speed by their hull length – the longer the waterline length, the greater the speed attainable. No amount of engine power can break this law. Designs typically feature a round bilge with or without a small keel to take grounding. They are slow but seaworthy, as the round bilge cushions the shock from the waves. They are, however, prone to a rolling motion. Displacement boats usually have one engine but two engines are not uncommon. You can calculate the maximum speed of a displacement boat: 1.4 x waterline length in feet.

Semi-displacement

A semi-displacement hull is a hybrid between planing and displacement hulls. It allows greater speed than a displacement hull and offers good sea keeping but does not fully plane. Because it does not fully plane, fuel consumption can be relatively high.

How rudders work

Rudders

A boat will only react to steering when there is water flowing over the rudder, just as a wheel will only steer a car if the tyre is moving along the road. Water flow over the rudder is gained in three ways: water flow from the propeller; the boat moving through the water; or a stream running over the rudder. Motorboat rudders are comparatively small and require a fast water flow from the propeller to achieve useful steerage. They therefore tend to steer effectively only if the boat is in gear.

Rudders work by deflecting water flow. Most motorboat rudders are small and ineffective without prop-wash from the propeller.

Rudder hard over then engine in gear will throw prop-wash over one side of the rudder, diverting the prop-wash and turning the boat.

When going astern, prop-wash does not flow across the rudder. Steering relies on water flow gained by motoring astern, but this is unlikely to be enough to give adequate steerageway because of the small surface area of the rudder blade.

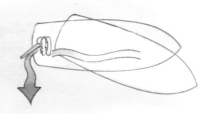

Top Tip

When manoeuvring in tight spaces, turn the rudder first and then apply power in short bursts. The prop-wash from the propeller deflects off the angled rudder and turns the boat.

Pivot points

When a boat turns, the bow goes one way and the stern the other. In fact, because of the position of the rudder, it is actually the stern of the boat that is being steered even though the bow is turning. The stern swings out to one side similar to a shopping trolley or wheelbarrow (to make the bow point in one direction, the stern is steered the opposite way). A wheelbarrow or shopping trolley pivots on it's front wheel and a boat is no different. It too has a pivot point. In fact it has two, when motoring ahead, the pivot point is roughly 1/3rd from the bow; when going astern, the pivot point moves back to roughly 1/3rd from the stern.

Beware of colliding with obstructions with your stern, as this has the greatest swing. When travelling ahead and turning to port, the stern swings to starboard. If the boat is 15 metres long. 10 metres swings to starboard and only 5 metres of bow initially turns to port.

In astern, the pivot point moves to a point roughly 1/3rd from the stern. On our hypothetical 15 metre boat, the bow has now become 10 metres in length and the stern only 5 metres. The forward 10 metres of the boat has little grip in the water because of its relative shallow draft and when reversing in wind the bow requires constant monitoring.

Propellers

Propellers – or, as they were first known, screws – push the boat through the water. There are many types of propeller and their exact design depends on the type of boat they are propelling. Props are measured by diameter and pitch. The pitch is the amount of twist in the prop, and is measured by the theoretical amount that it would drive forward for each revolution. A prop measuring 20in x 30in would be 20in diameter and would drive forwards 30in per revolution (fig 1).

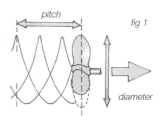

fig 1

Props are also 'handed' either right hand or left hand. This refers to which way it turns and the forward edge of the blade.

In forward gear this prop would twist or spin right-handed (clockwise) in astern gear it would spin anticlockwise (fig 2).

fig 2

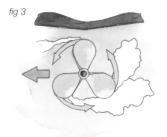

fig 3

Propwalk

Propellers push the boat forward, but because of their rotation they also make the stern move to one side. This effect is called prop-walk, because of the tendency of the prop to walk the stern to one side. It is most noticeable when going astern. Nearly all boats have prop-walk, and prop and hull design dictate its effect on the handling characteristics of the boat (fig 3).

Single screw

Going ahead

Boats are designed to go forward and their stream lined shape helps reduce prop-walk effect when motoring ahead. A right-hand prop walks the stern to starboard when going ahead whilst still providing forward motion. It may be necessary to steer slightly the other way to counteract this effect although in ahead the effect of propwalk is usually negligible.

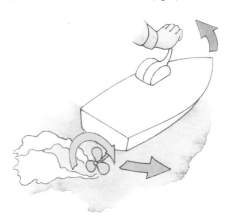

Going astern

Going astern, a right-handed prop will walk the stern to port. Prop-walk will always be more noticeable going astern. Some boats will walk around in a large circle whilst going astern, while others have negligible prop-walk and reverse in a straight line. In use, forward prop walk will be hardly noticed – the overriding effect on the boat will be the 'kick-to-port' in astern, and most close-quarter manoeuvres will be affected by this, especially on single prop vessels.

Check for prop-walk whilst tied alongside. Ensure the rudder is straight, engage astern gear and observe which side the wash comes out from under the hull. Wash to starboard suggests a kick to port in astern. It is useful to establish which way a single-prop boat kicks before manoeuvring out of the berth.

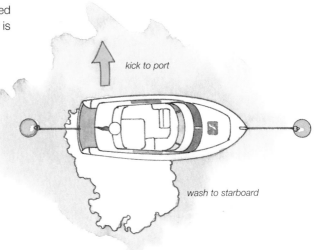

kick to port

wash to starboard

Twin screws

Most twin-screw boats use contra-rotating propellers. The propellers are placed equispaced either side of the centreline and are outward turning – rotating in contrary directions. When the engines are engaged one at a time they reinforce the pivoting action and increase the rate of turn. When both props are used in ahead the boat drives straight ahead.

Twin-screws allow excellent manoeuvrability when used independently or together.

1 Port engine in forward gear drives the bow to starboard.

2 Starboard engine in forward gear drives the bow to port.

3 Port engine astern drives the stern to starboard.

4 Starboard engine astern drives the stern to port.

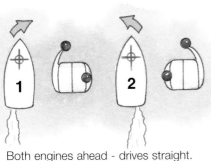

Both engines ahead - drives straight.

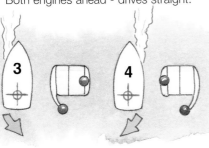

Outdrives

Outdrives are a steerable leg with a prop on the end. They are a very efficient way of directing power in the correct direction because the wheel steers the leg and the throttle adjusts the power. Because there is no rudder to divert prop-wash, steering is greatly enhanced when the prop is turning.

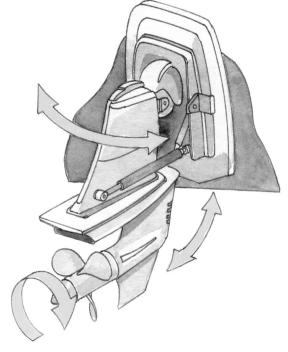

The outdrive leg is usually steered hydraulically – the hydraulic pump is belt-driven by the engine. The leg can be moved up and down using hydraulic rams, adjusting the boat's trim in the water when underway and allowing the leg to be raised clear of obstacles in shallow water or when not in use. Check hydraulic oil fluid levels regularly.

There are definite pros and cons with an inboard/outdrive installation.

Pros

- Shallow-water use possible because the outdrive lifts.

- Trim and steering in one package.

- Points thrust in desired direction.

- Easy-to-change prop.

Cons

- Gearbox in the sea at all times, leading to an increase in corrosion.

- Outdrives vulnerable when reversing in marinas.

- Rubber seal between engine and outdrive must be maintained.

Duoprop

Duoprop configuration has two contra-rotating props on one leg. This allows greater performance, elimination of prop-walk and quieter running. In effect the pitch is twice that of a normally propped boat, therefore it tries to drive forward twice as much for the same revs, improving the efficiency.

Outdrive legs are placed closer to the centreline of the boat than shafts so that the props are in the water at speed. This is a hindrance in close-quarter manoeuvring, as the two props do not exert as much pivoting force as shafts and require steering to help the turn.

Close-quarter boat handling on twin outdrive boats works according to the rule of opposites. If you want the boat to turn in a forward direction to port; turn the wheel to port and use the starboard engine ahead. If you want the boat to turn in a forward direction to starboard; put the wheel to starboard and use the port engine ahead, i.e. you use the engine opposite to the helm direction. The same applies in astern for most situations

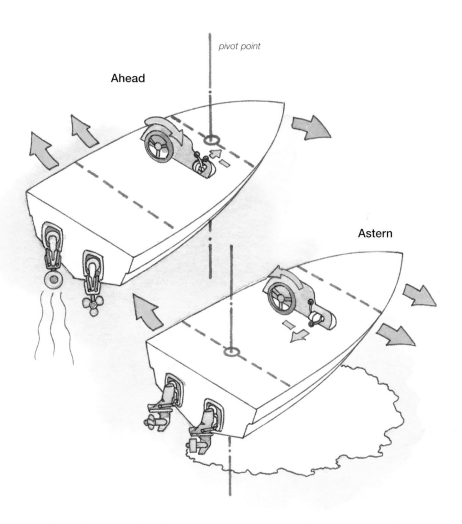

pivot point

Ahead

Astern

When determining the pivot point of an outdrive boat, the vessel is once again split up into thirds. However, the measurement starts from the end of the outdrive leg and this moves both pivot points further aft.

Single-prop outdrive boats may encounter prop-walk when driving forward; this is overcome by steering slightly the opposite way. Boats may have single, twin or even triple outdrives.

Bow thrusters

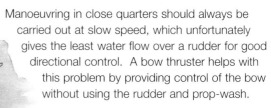

Manoeuvring in close quarters should always be carried out at slow speed, which unfortunately gives the least water flow over a rudder for good directional control. A bow thruster helps with this problem by providing control of the bow without using the rudder and prop-wash.

Essentially, it is a propeller assembly inserted into the bow of the boat to help control the bow in tight situations. Bow thrusters are powered by an electric or hydraulic motor, which drives a propeller housed in a tube at the bow. They are controlled from the helm position and when used in conjunction with a rudder and engines are a very useful tool.

Bow thrusters are useful for positioning the bow in light winds. Most are not powerful enough to push the bow into stronger winds, but they will slow the bows downwind drift. Most bow thrusters are not designed for continuous running and may automatically cut out as an overheat temperature or minimum battery voltage is reached - use in short bursts.

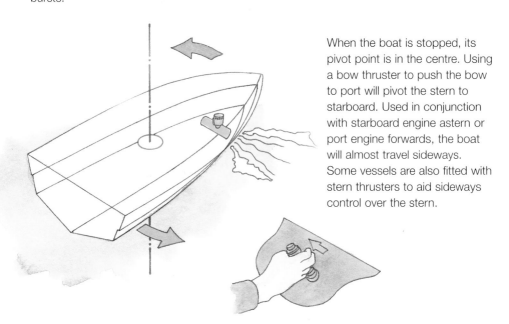

When the boat is stopped, its pivot point is in the centre. Using a bow thruster to push the bow to port will pivot the stern to starboard. Used in conjunction with starboard engine astern or port engine forwards, the boat will almost travel sideways. Some vessels are also fitted with stern thrusters to aid sideways control over the stern.

Before using a bow thruster control, ensure that it turns the bow the way that you assume. A control can be wired so that a toggle to starboard could indicate the bow moving to starboard or the push coming from starboard that would move the bow to port.

Many single-engine boats use bow thrusters, as these craft do not have the manoeuvrability which twin screws and outdrives provide. They should be thought of as an aid to perfection rather than as a cure for poor boathandling.

Effect of wind & stream

The forces of wind and stream have an effect on how the boat reacts when manoeuvring. Because planing motorboats have so much windage above the water and so little grip in the water, the wind can easily blow them across the water's surface. Displacement boats may be affected less by wind but more by stream.

Wind

Be aware of wind direction. Flags around the dock, wind indicators at the top of yacht masts and wind ruffling the surface of the water are all useful telltales. It is useful to fit a flag or wind indicator on a motorboat.

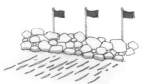

1

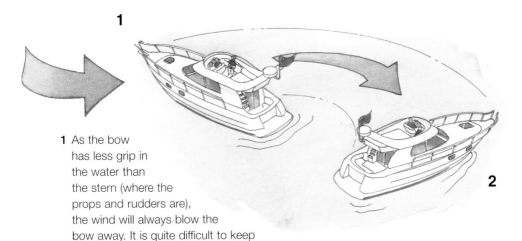

1 As the bow has less grip in the water than the stern (where the props and rudders are), the wind will always blow the bow away. It is quite difficult to keep a motor cruiser bow into wind for this reason. Left to lie naturally, it will sit beam to wind or with the wind on one quarter.

2

3

2 The effect wind has on a boat is twofold. Firstly, if the boat is moving slowly or has stopped, wind drifts the whole boat sideways. Sideways drift can be used to advantage in some coming-alongside techniques, but good spatial awareness is required if you are to avoid drifting downwind onto obstructions. Stalled motorboats may drift at 10% of the windspeed: 20 knot wind = 2 knots drift.

3 The easiest way to hold position in wind is to reverse gently and sit stern to wind. Reversing moves the pivot point aft. The stern can seek the wind and the bow is allowed to blow off downwind.

Streams

Streams are caused by either tide, natural river flow, or by local movement of water, as occurs around locks. Streams, have a similar effect as stepping onto a conveyor belt, they move you bodily in one direction.

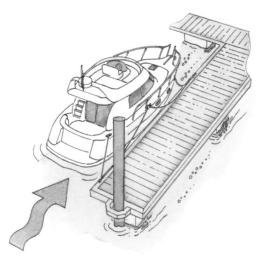

If you motor in the same direction as the stream, the boat travels faster over the ground and reaches its destination quicker. Motoring against the stream will take longer to reach your destination; even if you are travelling through the water at the same speed, your speed over ground will be less.

When coming alongside a pontoon a boat pointing into the stream is slower over ground whilst retaining good steerageway, this allows much more control.

Assessing stream direction

Stream can also push you onto or away from dangers. To assess the stream direction, look for its signs:

- Bubbles in the water flowing past a moored boat.

- Moored boat leaving a wake.

- Tight mooring lines indicating pressure from one side.

- Seaweed on the pontoon float flowing down-tide.

- Water stacking up around piles and buoys.

If you are still unsure of the streams direction, motor slowly across the channel and look ahead at two points in line to check for drift. It is worth noting that the stream can be less near the shore, and there is sometimes a reduction in rate in a marina or dock. When both wind and stream are opposing each other, assess which is the stronger by motoring slowly across the stream and gauging which way the boat is being pushed.

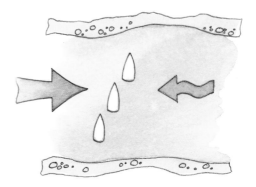

Turning 9

Each boat design has its own idiosyncrasies, but all are operated using the tools of engines, pivot points, rudder, prop-wash and prop-walk. These tools are used to counter the elements of wind and stream. Used wisely, wind and stream will make your boat handling easier; used unwisely, they conspire to push you onto dangers.

The secret to good turning is thinking through the turn before it is attempted and trying to use the elements to your advantage. If the elements of wind and stream are present, always turn the bow into them to reduce the chance of being swept downwind or downstream.

- Use the least possible revs: outdrives and twin-screws usually need only tick-over in gear.

- Single screws may require a short burst of power, but only when the rudder is hard over.

- Allow the gearshift to rest in neutral momentarily when changing between forward and astern to reduce the chance of crashing gears.

Turning a single screw boat

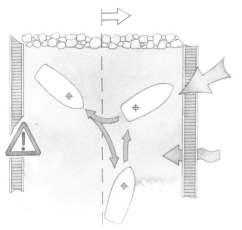

A single screw boat is turned using bursts of ahead and astern. These bursts are only applied when the wheel is turned hard over, so that the rudder deflects the burst of prop-wash straight away and its power is transmitted into the turn and not into forward progress. Typically a burst is 2 seconds, depending on conditions.

Position the boat in the centre of the space (shown in the diagram left). Start too close to the port side and the stern is in danger of clipping the pontoon.

Approach slowly – speed carried into a turn makes the turning circle larger.

Wheel hard over to starboard and give a burst ahead. Engage neutral.

Monitor both bow and stern to check they are clearing all obstacles. Watch the bow to monitor the rate of turn.

When the rate of turn slows or space ahead is limited, go astern. Changes in rudder position are ineffective as there is insufficient space to gain steerageway.

Momentum and prop-walk are now turning the boat.

Select neutral and monitor the turn.

Engage ahead and give another burst forward. Engage neutral.

The wheel should not have moved throughout and should still be hard over.

Once the correct direction is achieved, straighten the wheel and select tick-over ahead.

9 Turning

Turning a single-screw boat in wind

When turning in wind it is important to turn the bow through the wind. Once the bow is through, the wind will help blow the bow in the desired direction. Keep an eye on the wind direction.

Watch out for drift on your approach.

1 Wheel hard over to starboard and give a burst ahead. Engage neutral.

2 Monitor space forward and aft. Watch the wind direction – it is important to get the bow close to or through the wind.

3 When the rate of turn slows or space ahead is limited, go astern.

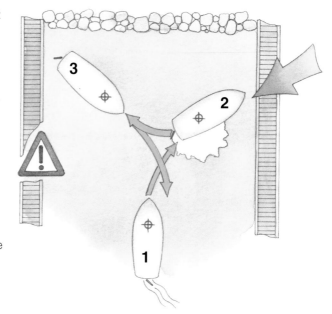

Be ready to go ahead again when space permits. The only way to get the bow through the wind is using the burst ahead. Once the bow has gone through the wind, the wind will pivot the bow.

Monitor space and drift.
When the correct direction is achieved, straighten the wheel.

Select tick-over ahead.

Top Tips

- Used to your advantage, prop-walk astern helps by walking the stern in a particular direction.

- In astern this boat with a right-handed propeller walks the stern to port.

- Rudder first, then power

- Pivot points – $1/3$ from the bow going ahead; $1/3$ from the stern going astern.

Twin-screw boats

Twin-screw boats are very manoeuvrable and may be turned in different ways:

Using a single engine either ahead or astern allows a gentle turn. Driving ahead on one engine at a time is a useful technique when motoring slowly around a marina or harbour as it allows slow speed with manoeuvrability.

Using one engine ahead and the rudder to divert the prop wash of the forward driving prop achieves a tighter turn.

An even tighter turn is achieved by using both throttles simultaneously. Using port engine ahead and starboard engine astern twists the boat around in her own length. Using both engines combined with wheel to starboard creates the smallest turn as the rudder diverts the prop-wash from the port engine.

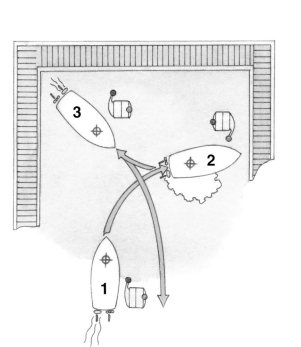

When learning to turn a twin-screw boat, it is easier to concentrate on just one throttle at a time. Each engine may be used independently to perform an adequate turn.

1 Motor slowly ahead using one engine at a time. Allow enough room for the stern to swing. Port engine tick-over ahead, until the boat runs out of room.

2 Select neutral on port engine and select starboard engine astern.

3 Select neutral on starboard engine, and use port engine ahead to complete the turn. Because each engine is used independently, more space is required to complete the turn.

Top Tips

- Pivot point 1/3 from the bow going ahead.
- Only tick-over is normally required.
- Rudder position increases the effect of the ahead driving engine.

9 Turning

Tighter turn

A tighter turn is achieved using the rudders and screws. The rudder is set up and left in the same position throughout the turn, as it is only effective with the engine driving ahead. This turn is still completed using one engine at a time, but the rudder increases the effectiveness of the forward-driving propeller.

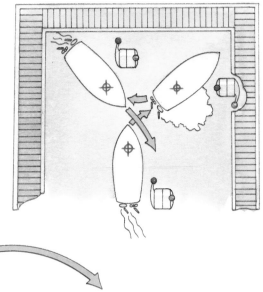

 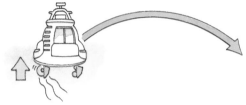

Split throttles

To create a tight turn, use one engine ahead and one astern. For an even tighter turn, use the rudder as well. Wheel hard over to starboard, port engine ahead, starboard engine astern and she should turn in her own length. Because the boat is designed to drive forward, it may creep forward during the turn, making it necessary to take the forward engine out of gear momentarily. It is always better to decrease revs, or take an engine out of gear, rather than to increase revs.

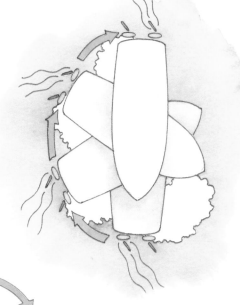

Turning an outdrive

Turning with outdrives requires constant use of the wheel, because the wheel controls the direction of the prop-wash. To achieve the tightest turn, the wheel should be turned before the prop is engaged so that the prop-wash induces the turn and does not use up valuable turning space by driving it forward first. Wash from the prop driving astern is also directional and is used to help the turn.

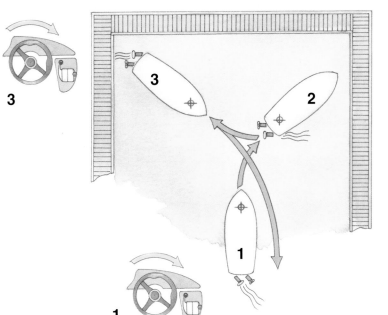

The order goes like this:
Neutral – turn wheel – ahead – neutral – reverse wheel –astern. Repeat the sequence until the turn is completed.

Motor slowly into the space.
Slow the boat.
1 Wheel hard over to starboard.
  Ahead port engine.
  Monitor the turn.
2 Neutral when space is short.
  Wheel hard over to port.
  Astern starboard engine.
  Monitor turn.
3 Neutral when space is short.
  Wheel hard over to starboard.
  Ahead port engine.
  Monitor turn.
  Straighten helm when turn completed.

The diagram features twin outdrives. If only a single is fitted, use the same wheel movements.

In all cases, the pivot point on outdrive boats is further back when going astern. This has the effect of making the bow drift very quickly when reversing in a cross wind. If the bow does start drifting uncontrollably, let it, and the stern will seek the wind. Reverse into the wind to make more space, and then recover the manoeuvre by motoring forward.

Top Tips

- Use opposite wheel lock to engine – wheel to starboard, use port engine.
- Pivot points are further aft on an outdrive.
- Change wheel position between motoring ahead and astern.

10 Berthing

Preparing to come alongside

Successful coming alongside calls for good communication and briefing. Assess the strength and direction of wind and stream. Make a plan and inform the crew exactly what you want them to do. If the manoeuvre looks complicated, drawing it out on a scrap of paper can make a seemingly complex situation quite straightforward. Consider making a dummy run to check your decision. Have an escape plan.

Have warps and fenders ready and check the warps are led properly. Fender the beam but also the extremities of bow and stern, as these may touch the pontoon first.

If you do not feel happy with your approach, go around again.

Power use

Normally, tick-over ahead or astern is all that's required. Twin-screw boats can use one engine at a time to keep their speed low. Single-screw boats may need to use short bursts of power, but only when the wheel is hard over to help a turn. Whenever manoeuvring, remember: wheel first, then power. This ensures that the rudder is in the correct position before the prop-wash hits it and starts the turn.

On your approach, drop in and out of gear to check how much way the boat carries through the water. Check that reverse works.

> ### Top Tip
>
> If a collision is unavoidable, remember:
>
> Excess power in close quarters only makes matters worse.
>
> High Power = Insurance claim
>
> Low power + Fenders = A close encounter...

Judging your progress

When you are close to the pontoon, it is sometimes difficult to judge the final distance, so ask the crew to relay the distance-off by voice or hand signals. Ensure both you and the crew are working in the same units of measurement.

Speed

It is easy to become too focused on the pontoon that you are heading for and not notice the boat is drifting sideways or moving too fast. Your speed should be judged not by electronic log, but relative to the pontoon that you're coming alongside. Look around especially ahead to enable you to judge movement and speed. To gauge speed, monitor the rate you pass fixed objects abeam, such as cleats, piles or moored boats.

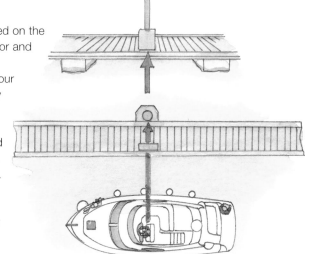

Drift

Because wind may blow you on or off the pontoon, your drift should also be assessed. Use transits (two fixed objects in line) to check your course over ground. If the wind is blowing you off the pontoon, you will need to counteract its force by aiming more at the pontoon. If the wind is blowing you onto the pontoon you will need to counteract its force by aiming away. If your approach does not feel right, go around again or back away from the situation and take another run.

Essential rope work

Lassoing

Some motorboats are too high-sided to easily step ashore with a warp when coming alongside. Instead of trying to jump down onto the pontoon to get warps ashore, the crew can lasso the cleat instead.

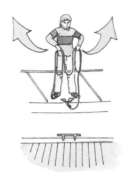
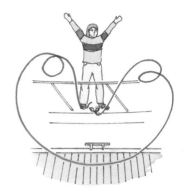

Attach one end of a mooring warp to a cleat on the boat. Lead the mooring warp underneath the guardrails and coil the warp into loops. Extend the loose end and either hold or stand on it. Split the coils so that there are equal amounts in each hand.

When the chosen dockside cleat is near, throw the coils out and over it. Lead the loose end to a cleat on board and take a turn. Pull in any slack and secure; practice this when the boat is moored, before you have to do it for real.

Taking a turn and securing

Because large loads can come onto a warp, keep fingers a safe distance away from the cleat.

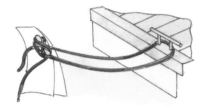

Take a full turn around the cleat – this takes the load of the boat whilst still allowing the warp to be eased or taken in.

A figure of eight takes more strain…

…then two more turns complete the sequence – the boat is now secure and the cleat may be left.

Slip lines

Before leaving, rig the bow and stern lines so that they can be slipped from the boat. Lead a line from the boat around a cleat ashore and back to the boat again. Keep the short end on top so that the line is quicker to slip – this also reduces the likelihood of a stern warp going around the propeller.

Top Tip

Keep the boat stationary and allow no load to come onto the lines, until fingers are clear of cleats.

Always check that lines are led correctly before coming alongside.

Mooring alongside

Floating pontoon

The most common mooring, especially in marinas and docks, is a pontoon. This will rise and fall with the height of the water; so the boat is made fast without any allowance for water height.

The ends of the mooring warps are attached to the cleats ashore then adjusted and tightened from the boat. Bow and stern lines keep the boat alongside the pontoon. Spring lines adjust its fore and aft movement.

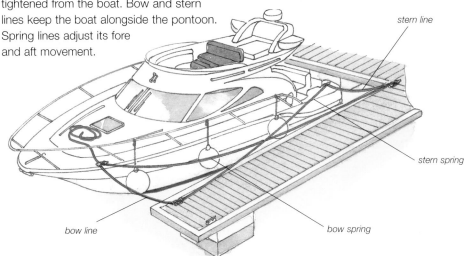

stern line

stern spring

bow line

bow spring

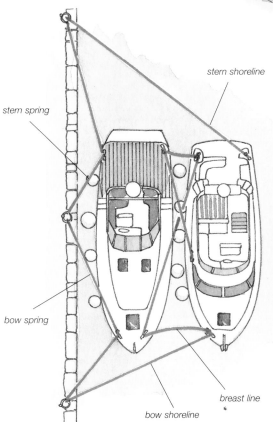

stern spring

stern shoreline

bow spring

bow shoreline

breast line

Rafting

Rafting up alongside another boat calls for extra lines attached to the shore. These shorelines should take the load and not the breast ropes connecting you to the other vessel. Ensure your fenders are at the correct height to protect both boats.

Manners

When rafted up, walk across the front of a neighbouring boat to go ashore.

Tidy up the lines and keep the excess line on board the boat and not on the pontoon.

Take down the ensign at night when moored between the hours of 2100 and 0800 BST or 2100-0900 GMT or at dusk in lighter months.

If it is late, go inside to talk so that you do not wake the crews of other boats.

Move outside the raft if you are planning an early departure.

Ask what time your neighbour is planning to leave so that you can be around if required.

A harbour wall

Allowing for tidal rise and fall

To compensate for the rise and fall of the tide, all lines ashore should be a length no less than four times the range of tide. This allows a scissor-like action that keeps the boat close to the wall. Ensure the lines are led outside guardrails and stanchions so that they will not catch as the tide falls and puts strain on the fittings or hang the boat.

Mooring warps are best made of nylon – this possesses good stretch properties that reduce the shock load on the boat.

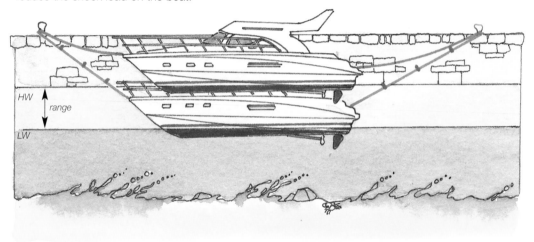

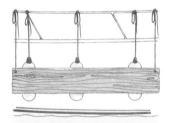

A fender board is required to spread the load of the fenders around the pile or wall. Many harbours supply their own fender boards, whereas in other areas it is wise to carry your own.

Coming alongside

When coming alongside, the approach should be into current or wind, as these elements slow the boat. The power of the current should never be underestimated. Motoring into a 2 knot current at 2 knots boat speed allows good water flow over the rudder, giving steerage without the boat actually moving over ground.

The type of boat you operate dictates how you actually come alongside the pontoon. Twin-shaft boats and outdrives are able to connect the bow or stern to the pontoon using a lasso, and then pivot the boat alongside using the outside engine. Single-shaft boats need boat speed and water flowing over the rudder for steerage – they are therefore continually in and out of gear while steering the boat alongside.

Single-shaft approach.

- Rig a bow and stern line, plus a line from the beam. The beam line is connected to a cleat ashore to hold her alongside while the other lines are attached.

- Make a shallow approach, aiming halfway along the available gap. Motor slowly towards the pontoon using tick-over or neutral with a straight wheel.

- When the bow is one metre away, steer the bow away from the pontoon and engage forward gear for a short time. This swings the stern in to bring her alongside.

- Give a burst astern to stop. The line led from the beam is attached to the pontoon first, followed by bow then stern line.

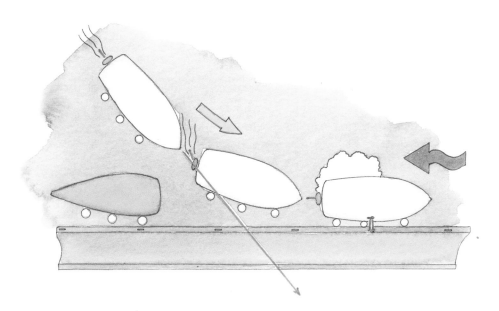

Twin-shaft approach

Identify the cleat by which the bow will sit when you are alongside.

1 Using one engine at a time, motor slowly towards the cleat.

2 When the cleat is close, stop the boat, engage neutral and lasso the cleat with the bow line. Take up any slack in the lasso line and secure.

3 Engage tick-over astern on the outside engine. This action pulls back on the bow line and pivots the stern towards the pontoon. When the stern is close to the pontoon, secure.

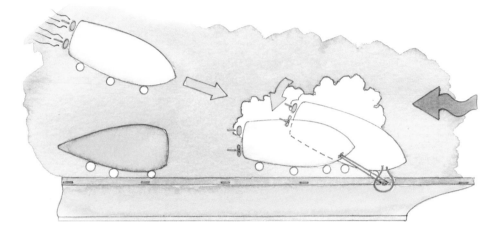

Outdrive approach

Using a combination of one engine and wheel, slowly motor towards a cleat where the bow will rest once you are alongside.

- Stop the boat.
- Lasso the cleat, take up the slack and secure.
- Steer towards the pontoon and engage the outside engine in astern.
- Secure the stern line once the stern is close to the pontoon.
- Single outdrive boats can use the same technique.

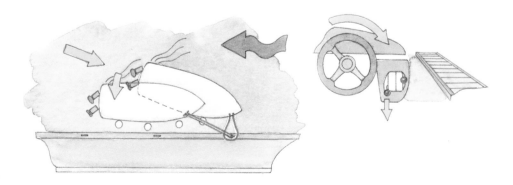

Berthing, in onshore and offshore winds

The wind blowing the boat onto or away from the pontoon makes a difference to the approach we make when coming alongside. If the wind is onshore – blowing onto the pontoon – it will blow the boat alongside. An offshore wind makes the approach a little trickier as the wind is blowing the boat away from the pontoon.

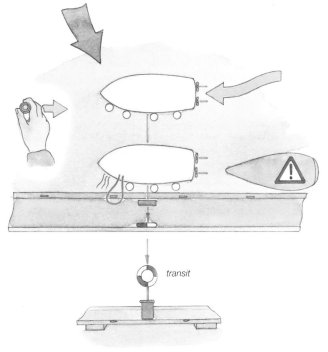

transit

Onshore wind arrival
Twin-screw

Twin screws combined with an onshore wind allow the boat to move sideways. It will, however, move downwind sideways towards anything in its path, be it the pontoon or, if positioned wrongly, other moored boats.

- Ensure the gap is large enough by taking a dummy run. Fender the side well.

- Motor parallel to the gap.

- Once lined up, pick a transit to ensure the boat does not move fore and aft.

- Control your drift using the engines. Outside engines take you into the gap whilst inside engines slow your drift for a softer landing.

- A bow thruster can be used to reduce the bow's rate of drift towards the pontoon.

Outdrive and single-screw

Note: The bow on outdrive boats blows away very easily.

To ensure the boat arrives parallel alongside the pontoon it is often necessary to steer the bow into the wind away from the pontoon on the initial approach. Because forward power is used to maintain the approach angle, it is necessary to start the approach earlier than with a twin screw.

- Angle the bow away from the pontoon.

- Use small nudges of ahead to maintain this angle as the wind pushes the boat alongside. Twin outdrives may use their inside engine combined with the wheel to hold the boat up-wind.

- Monitor the stern to ensure that it passes any dangers.

- As the boat closes the pontoon, allow the bow to drift alongside. If a bow thruster is fitted, use it to reduce drift.

Offshore wind arrival

When the wind is blowing the boat off the pontoon, it is necessary to make a more positive approach and at a greater angle to counter the wind force. Fender the bow area well.

Twin-screw

Approach the pontoon maintaining steerageway against the wind using one engine at a time. The outside engine will help steer the bow towards the pontoon when it is near. In strong winds it may be necessary to motor at right angles towards the pontoon.

Lasso the cleat where the bow will be positioned and cleat off.

There are now three ways to bring the stern close to the pontoon, depending on wind strength.

a) Light offshore wind: go astern on the outside engine as normal.

b) Moderate offshore wind: go astern on the outside engine, whilst using touches of ahead on the inside engine – similar to turning the boat around. This also takes some load off the lassoed cleat.

c) Strong offshore wind: go astern on the outside engine, use touches of ahead on the inside engine and turn the wheel away from the pontoon. This diverts prop-wash from the inside engine over the rudder, turning the stern towards the pontoon.

d) Larger boats may need to go ahead on the inside engine as well as astern on the outside engine; to reduce the load on the cleat.

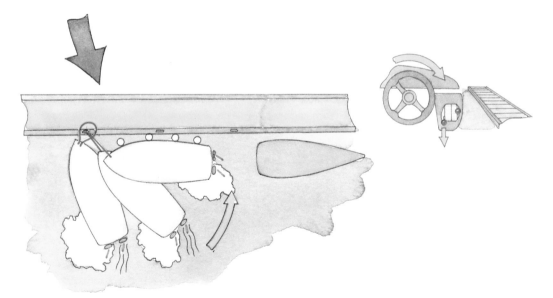

Outdrives

• Approach the pontoon and lasso the cleat.

• Steer towards the pontoon and go astern on the outside engine.

• Once the stern is close, secure the stern line.

• If the stern is coming in too quickly, reduce the amount of wheel.

Single-screw

A single-screw boat is motored alongside the pontoon in one flowing approach. Unfortunately, the outdrive and twin-screw techniques of reversing on a bow line are ineffective to help a single screw boat alongside. The single screw approach is more direct and positive.

- Aim at the first third of the gap. Choose a transit forward to assess whether you are drifting sideways on your approach.

- When the bow is about one metre off, steer away from the pontoon and engage forward gear to bring in the stern.

- As the stern closes the pontoon, go astern to stop the boat.

- A line rigged from the beam will help keep the boat alongside while bow and stern lines are attached.

Prop walk can influence which side you berth to, as it will kick the stern either towards or away from the pontoon.

Warp assisted

Single screw boats may find using these lines to come alongside will ease the manouvre.

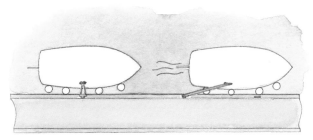

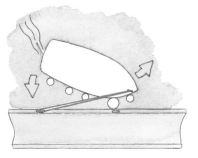

A line from the beam can hold her alongside.

Gently motor ahead on a line from the beam to hold her alongside.

Motor gently ahead against a bow spring whilst steering the bow away from the pontoon

General principles on leaving a berth

To leave a berth, we can use of the curvature of the bow to enable the stern to come away from the dock. Once the stern is in clear water, we can steer the boat away from the dock.

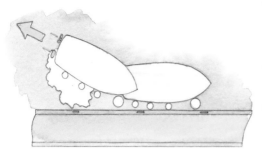

Twin screw

- Protect the bow area with fenders and go astern with the inside prop.

- This pivots the stern away from the pontoon whilst also reversing the boat out.

- Once the stern is angled away from the pontoon, the outside engine can be used to straighten the boat and help the exit.

Outdrives

- Outdrives use a different technique.

- Steer away from the dock and go astern using the outside engine.

- This has the tendency to lift the boat off the dock sideways.

- This is the one exception to the rule of opposites, where we can for instance use helm to port and port engine astern.

Single screw

- To get the stern in clear water, motor the bow towards the dock.

- Ensure the bow area is fendered well. Turn the wheel towards the dock, and then engage tick-over ahead for a second or two. This pivots the stern into clear water. Select neutral, straighten the wheel and go astern.

Leaving a berth - offshore wind

An offshore wind assists your exit. Rig bow and stern slip lines. Pick a transit abeam to monitor movement. Slip the stern line, followed by the bow line. The stern is slipped first as it has more grip in the water and takes longer to drift away – the bow will quickly follow.

Leaving a berth - onshore wind

Just as we have motored against lines to help us alongside a pontoon, we can also use them again to get off.

Twin screw

1 Twin screws and outdrives use a bow-line lasso rigged as a slip line. Tick-over astern on the inside engine pulls back on the bow line and slowly walks the stern into clear water. When the stern is clear, engage neutral, slip the lasso and reverse away.

If there is more wind, use the inside engine astern, turn the wheel to the dock, and engage the outside engine ahead. This pivots the stern away from the dock.

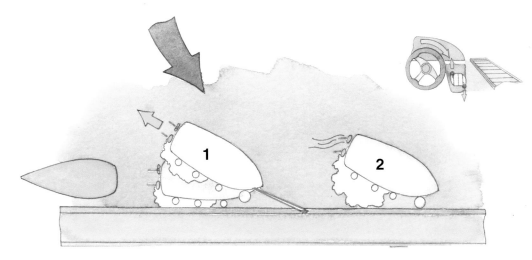

2 With practice, twin-screw boats often leave the pontoon without using any lines at all. Fender the bow well, steer towards the pontoon and use inside engine astern and small amounts of the outside engine in forward. Once the stern is in clear water, use both engines astern to drag the boat out of the gap.

Leaving a berth - outdrives

When the wind is pinning the boat on, it may require more than simply being lifted off the pontoon as stated earlier. Return to the law of opposites, steer away from the pontoon and use the inside engine to pivot on the bow line.

- Fender the bow area well.
- Rig a bow line so that it will slip easily from the boat.
- Steer away from the pontoon.
- Engage astern on the inside engine.
- When the stern is sufficiently away from the dock slip the bow line.
- It may be necessary to engage both engines astern and straighten the wheel depending on local obstructions and wind strength.

Bow thrusters

Bow thrusters can be very useful on single, twin screw and outdrive boats. They are not always powerful enough to bring the bow off a pontoon on very windy days, but should be capable in normal conditions. Sometimes it is worth waiting for a lull in the wind and then giving it a go.

- Fender the quarter and swim platforms well using the largest fenders.
- Slip both bow and stern lines.
- Apply the bow thruster (fig A) and watch what happens (outdrives boats should ensure the drives do not pivot into the pontoon).
- If the bow comes away (fig B) from the pontoon go ahead with a straight rudder.

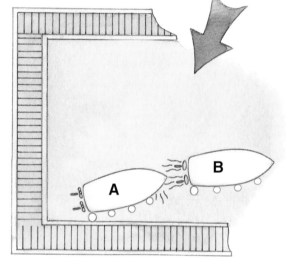

Twin screws and outdrives may help the bow thruster by going astern on the outside engine and, ahead on the inside engine to open up a gap at the bow. It is usual to go ahead briefly on both engines with a straight wheel to get the boat bodily away from the dock. If the inside engine is used independently it pivots the stern into the dock once again.

Leaving a Berth - single screw

Single-screw boats motor against a spring line to prise either the bow or the stern away from the pontoon. When one end of the boat is pointing away from the pontoon, the line is slipped and the boat drives away. Because of the natural curvature of the bow, the usual spring to use is a bow spring line on which the boat motors forward, diagram top right.

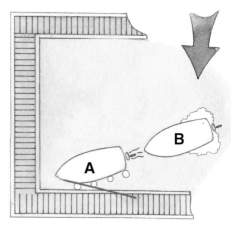

- Rig a bow spring slip line (fig A) and fender the bow area well.
- Ensure the spring runs directly from the bow cleat or fairlead onboard to a cleat situated amidships on the pontoon. A bad lead will pressure stanchions and fittings.
- Slip the stern line
- Gently drive forward to pivot the stern away from the pontoon.
- When the stern is in clear water, engage neutral.
- Slip the spring line (fig B) and reverse away.

Twin-screw and outdrive boats can also use this method.

Using springs in tide

To decide whether to use a bow or stern spring, check out the tide. Use the spring that allows the tide to help push you away from the dock.

When the stream is coming from ahead as (fig C) below, use a stern spring:

- Fender the quarter well, especially bathing platforms, as these are vulnerable and can get caught underneath the pontoon.
- Rig a stern spring slip line.
- Slip the bow line and go astern gently until the bow pivots away from the pontoon.
- The tide will also now help by pushing the bow away from the pontoon.
- When the bow is clear, engage neutral, slip the spring and motor ahead.

When the stream is coming from astern (fig D) use a bow spring:

- Fender the bow.
- Rig a bow spring slip line.
- Slip the stern and go ahead gently until the stern pivots away from the pontoon.
- The tide will help push the stern away once again.
- When the stern is clear, engage neutral, slip the spring and reverse out of the gap.

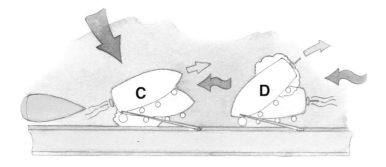

Marinas

Marina aisle

The close proximity of other boats requires precise handling in marinas and good communication.

Before leaving a marina berth, take stock of the conditions. Observe the wind direction and look for signs of stream. Stream is stronger in deep water, usually near the entrance to the marina aisle, so walk to the end pontoons to check the strength and direction.

Wind and stream information are used to determine the safe side of the marina aisle and which side poses danger. In the drawing the elements of wind and stream are pushing the boat to the left, which is the danger side. The boat is travelling on the right hand side to stay upstream and upwind of the danger.

Find a transit to ensure the boat is not drifting to one side. It may be necessary to counteract the elements by steering more to the right, in effect, crabbing out of the aisle. Twin-screw boats can use their downstream or downwind engine to keep speed down.

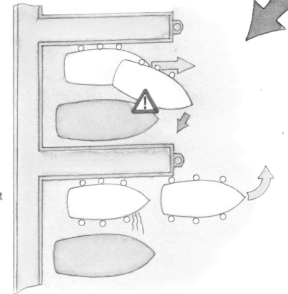

Leaving a berth

The bow is easily blown off and can hit a neighbouring boat, therefore always fender both sides well and rig slip lines to ease your departure.

If the wind is blowing you off the berth let the stern slip first to keep the bow upwind. Exit the berth positively, so that the wind does not drift you towards your neighbouring boat. Make sure the stern is clear of the neighbouring boat before turning, to avoid catching it. A bow thruster can be used to hold you upwind.

Marinas – arrival

If visiting, call the harbourmaster on the VHF for a berth.

When deciding your approach into a pontoon, position the boat so that you can see all of the pontoon. This is called making the pontoon open. An open pontoon allows the boat to slide into the berth, whereas if you attempt to enter a closed pontoon as fig A in the diagram below, the boat slides away from the berth.

Brief the crew and organise lines and fenders. Where the wind is blowing you off the berth there is a chance that you could end up alongside your neighbour, so fender both sides. Before you enter the marina, establish which is the safe side and how you might turn around and escape.

Approach on the safe side of the marina aisle, staying upwind or upstream. Turn the boat around and start your approach to the pontoon. Start your approach from the safe side and monitor your drift.

The wind is blowing off the pontoon so start from downwind and stay close to the pontoon on your approach. Lasso the bow cleat as fig B in the diagram below. Engage tick-over astern on the outside engine until the boat is parallel alongside. Secure the stern line.

In strong wind conditions it is better to fender both sides of the boat and aim to come alongside the downwind boat, instead of being accidentally blown onto it as fig C in the diagram below. It is a simple matter to walk lines to the pontoon and pull her across or motor astern on a bow line.

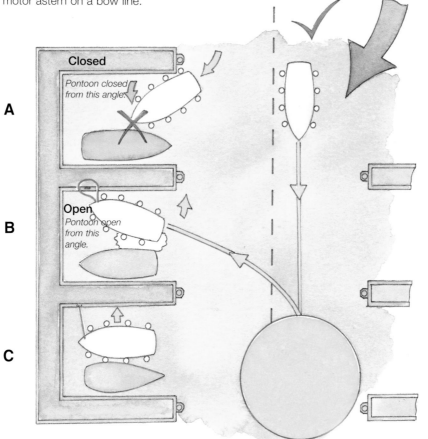

A

Closed

Pontoon closed from this angle.

Open

Pontoon open from this angle.

B

C

Putting the boat away when not in use

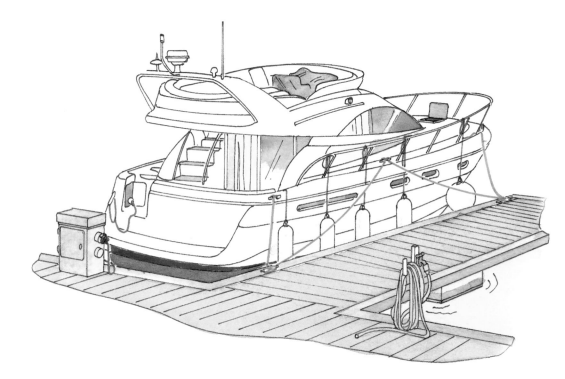

- Reduce revs approaching the marina to let the engine and turbochargers cool down.

- Keep fuel tanks topped up to stop condensation.

- Look in the engine compartment for leaks.

- Dry damp gear before storage to stop mould.

- Open hatches and cupboards to air the boat.

- Connect shore power.

- Check lines.

- Close curtains to stop woodwork fading.

- Rinse off decks and topsides.

- Check lines and fender placement.

- List any defects/breakdowns and organise replacements.

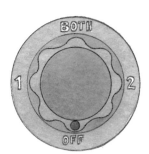

- Isolate or switch off batteries.

Locks 11

Locks allow a boat to go up or down a hill. In tidal waters, locks guard the entrance to harbours and basins that would otherwise dry out at low water. Tidal locks are operated by lockmasters and controlled by a traffic-light system to indicate whether the lock is in use. Lockmasters are usually contacted on VHF prior to arrival.

On inland waterways, a series of locks allows a boat to ascend a long incline and these tend to be manually operated. (The RYA Inland Waterways Handbook gives more information on locks.)

Many locks are narrow and possibly crowded with other vessels, rig fenders and lines on both sides. They may have a pontoon that rises with the water level to tie up to, or it may be necessary to attach lines to a riser bar or bollard.

Use caution approaching a lock and watch out for cross-streams which could drift the boat to one side. Wind funnels into a lock, increasing wind strength.

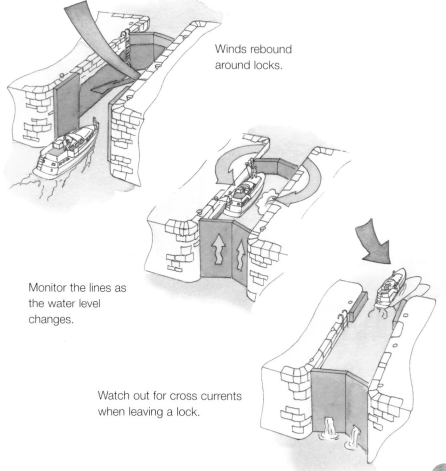

Winds rebound around locks.

Monitor the lines as the water level changes.

Watch out for cross currents when leaving a lock.

Types of anchor

Bruce

Good holding-to-weight ratio – self stows on some bow-roller systems. Awkward to stow in small anchor lockers.

Delta

Good holding-to-weight ratio – self-launches and self-stows. Awkward to stow in small lockers.

Danforth

Good holding-to-weight ratio in straight-line pull, but may break out and not reset if pulled from another direction. Difficult to handle because of moving parts Stows flat.

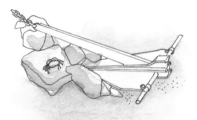

Plough/CQR

Good holding-to-weight ratio – relocates well. If stowed on bow, moving parts may need securing.

Fisherman

Good holding in rock and weed but needs to be 30% heavier than other types of anchor. Poor holding in sand and mud.

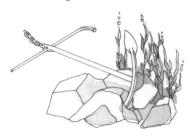

Scope

Scope is the amount of chain or warp let into the water. The amount of scope depends on the depth of water and whether chain or warp is used.

If warp is used, ensure 5-10m of chain is connected between anchor and warp. The chain acts as a cushion, helping to reduce the action of the boat pulling the anchor free.

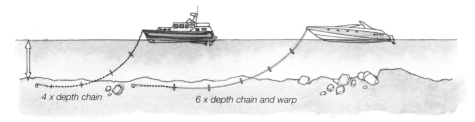

4 x depth chain   *6 x depth chain and warp*

All boats lie differently to the wind or stream, so allow plenty of swinging room. Yachts with deep keels will lie with the stream, while flat-bottomed motorboats will lie to the wind.

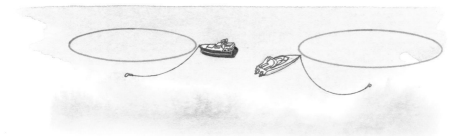

Two anchors

Boats should have two sets of anchoring equipment and chain/rope: a large main anchor at the bow, and a smaller one kept in a locker for emergencies. The second anchor is used to increase holding power in heavy weather or to reduce the swinging circle taken up in an anchorage.

Selecting an anchorage

Select an anchorage protected from the wind and swell. Ideally, the wind will be blowing out of the anchorage.

Observe how other vessels are lying or assess the conditions of wind and tide to decide how you will lie.

In tidal waters, work out the depth of water expected for the duration of your stay and select a location with adequate water.

Check the forecasted weather to see whether it will still offer protection when the wind changes.

If there is the slightest chance of bad weather, plan an escape route. It should take into account leaving the anchorage by day or by night.

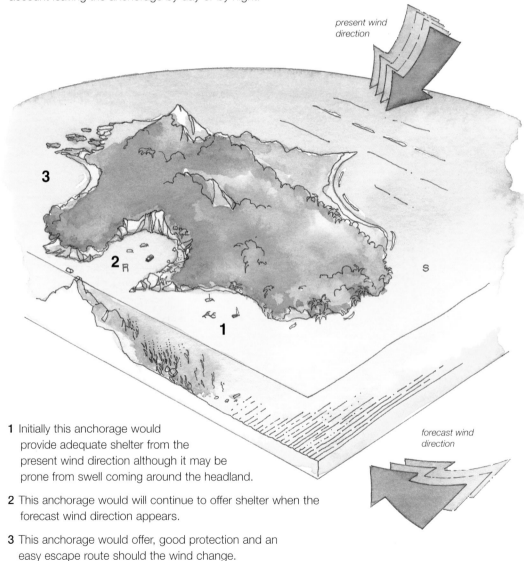

present wind direction

forecast wind direction

1 Initially this anchorage would provide adequate shelter from the present wind direction although it may be prone from swell coming around the headland.

2 This anchorage would will continue to offer shelter when the forecast wind direction appears.

3 This anchorage would offer, good protection and an easy escape route should the wind change.

Dropping anchor

- Switch on the windlass and disconnect ties or pins securing the anchor.

- Point the boat into the strongest element (wind or stream) and stop the boat movement over the ground. Lower the anchor to the seabed before the boat moves backwards.

- Continue easing the chain as the boat drifts back.

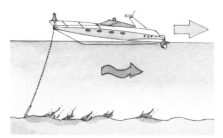

- If the conditions are calm, use tick-over astern to reverse.

- Once the anchor is laid, engage tick-over astern to dig in the anchor and ensure good holding.

- A windlass is rarely designed to take the load of a boat at anchor, so use a chain hook or attach a separate warp to the chain and lead to a cleat or strongpoint.

Avoid dropping all of the chain at once, as the chain lands on top of the anchor and fouls it.

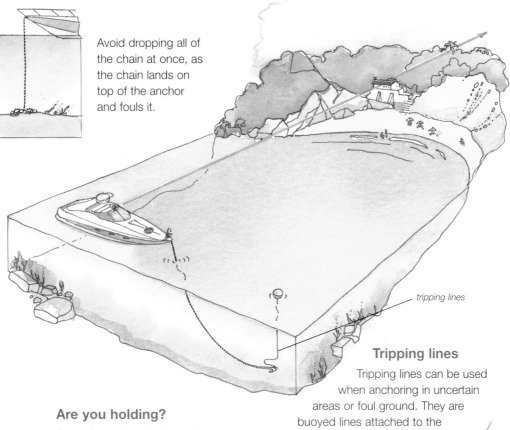

tripping lines

Are you holding?

Once the anchor is down, choose a transit abeam to check the anchor is holding. At the change of the tide and at nightfall, be prepared to pick new transits. Echo sounder and GPS alarms can be set to alert you of depth or position changes.

Tripping lines

Tripping lines can be used when anchoring in uncertain areas or foul ground. They are buoyed lines attached to the forward edge of the anchor to raise the anchor if it is snagged.

Weighing anchor

- Ask a crew member to point in the direction of the chain to help the helmsman steer towards it.

- Ensure that both your crew and helm, understand the hand signals.

- Use the windlass to raise the anchor chain. Motor slowly forwards to relieve the pressure on the chain, whilst taking up the slack using the windlass.

- Secure the anchor while the boat is in sheltered water.

- Switch the windlass off when anchor is raised.

1 A direct upwards pull should break the anchor out.

2 If not, secure the chain and motor gently forwards until it breaks free.

Once the anchor is up, let the helm know.

Stay in sheltered water until the anchor is secure and the crew are back in the cockpit and safe.

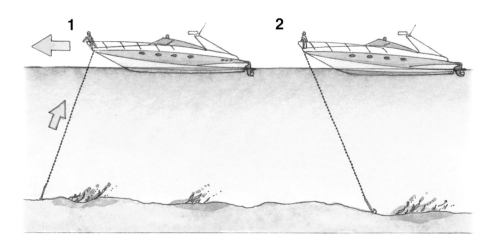

Top Tip

Monitor the wind

If the wind increases, let out more chain or warp to relieve the load on the anchor and to keep the pull as near horizontal as possible. A horizontal pull helps dig the anchor in further whereas a vertical pull lifts the anchor out.

Types of mooring

Special moorings - stern-to

Mooring in many areas is either stern-to or bows-to the quay. Motorboats usually moor stern-to the quay for ease of access to the shore. Stern lines are used to stay close to the quay, Whilst a passerelle or wooden plank, carried by the boat, is used to go ashore. The boat is held away by an anchor or a line sunk by the harbour authority.

The approach - stern-to using the anchor

Rig up fenders both sides and a large fender on the stern. Rig stern lines from both quarters.

- Prepare the anchor to drop.
- About four boat lengths away from the quay, drop the anchor and ease out the chain.
- One boat length from the quay, stop easing the chain so that the anchor digs in. Be ready to ease out more chain to reach the dock if required.
- Connect the windward stern line to shore, followed by the leeward stern line.
- Once positioned, the correct distance from the quay, take the strain up on the chain.

Crosswinds

In a crosswind, it may be necessary to reverse into wind initially to get steerageway. When slightly upwind of the gap, drop the anchor and reverse into the space. Ensure the leeward side is well fendered in case you drift onto the downwind boat.

Onshore wind

If the wind is on the bow, treat the stern-to mooring as a normal anchoring exercise. Drop the anchor four-boat lengths out and gently reverse into the gap with the stern lines ready. One boat length away from the quay, snub the anchor so that it digs in, then ease back and connect the stern lines.

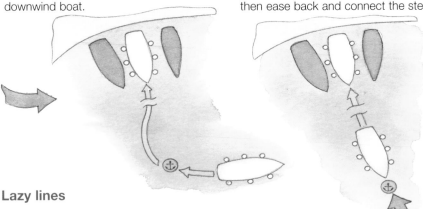

Lazy lines

Lazy lines are used in tight harbours and marinas where it would imprudent to drop the anchor because of the probability of it becoming fouled. Instead of the anchor holding the bow away, the bow is connected to a heavy bow line, which is attached to a concrete block. The bow line is also attached to a lighter line, which is led to the quayside for ease of retrieval.

The approach

- Rig up fenders either side and at the stern.
- Rig two stern lines.
- Reverse towards the quay.
- Connect windward stern line to quay.

- Pick up lazy line, lead to bow and make fast.
- Connect second stern line.
- Adjust bow and stern lines.

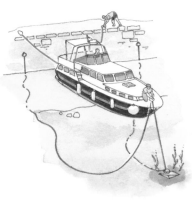

Top Tip

It is possible to hold the boat in position once the windward stern-line is attached by using small nudges ahead on the leeward engine.

Pen moorings

- Piles can also be used to keep a boat off the dock in a mooring pen. Lines are attached to the dock, and two stern lines, connected to piles, hold the boat away.

- Rig up two bow lines and two stern lines.

- Lead the windward stern line to the beam.

- The windward lines are attached first to stop the boat drifting.

- Depending on the space between the piles, fenders may or may not be used.

- Motor towards the windward pile and place a stern line over the pile. Do the same with the leeward pile if time and crew strength permit.

- Motor forwards and attach the bow lines, windward line first.

- Position the boat by easing the bow and pulling in on the stern.

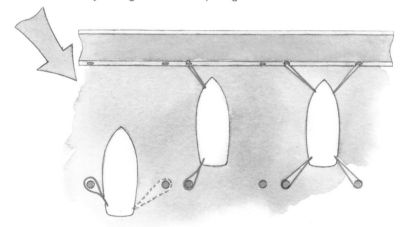

Sometimes, one of the piles is replaced by a pontoon for ease of access to the shore. This allows the boat to be held away from the pontoon by tightening up on the pile line and the corresponding line astern. Pick up lines are usually supplied on the piles to aid retrieval.

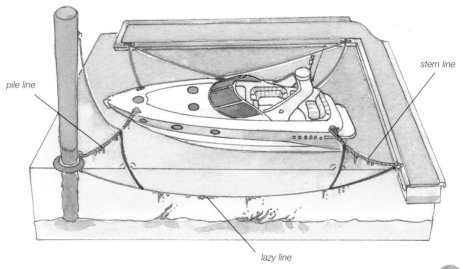

pile line

stern line

lazy line

Mooring buoys and piles

Picking up a mooring buoy requires good communication between the helmsman and crew. The mooring buoy disappears from sight when it gets close to the bow, so ask the crew to give directions by voice or hand signal. Pointing with the boat hook is a good visual aid.

pick-up buoy

Take a dummy run to establish the type of buoy. Some have pick-up buoys attached and are picked up using a boat hook. Others just have rings and are initially lassoed until secure lines are attached to the ring.

If in doubt of the approach angle: Assess the conditions of wind and tide by motoring slowly across the stream, then approach into the strongest element. Look at similarly moored boats to decide your approach angle. If there is no stream, approach into the wind.

If motoring into stream with a crosswind, stay slightly upwind to allow for drift as the boat slows down. Approach slowly and judge speed by looking at fixed objects abeam.

Hold the boat in position while the crew lasso or catch the pick-up buoy. The pick-up buoy is connected to a light line that is attached to a heavier mooring line. Pull this on board and make fast. Some cleats are too small to accept the heavy mooring line and it may be necessary to attach your own warps to the heavy line.

Lasso

When no pick-up line is present, use a lasso to catch the buoy, and then connect a line through the ring on top of the buoy.

Do not, under any circumstances, rest on a lasso line as it can pull the buoy off the chain. Secure one or two lines to the ring so that the boat stays central.

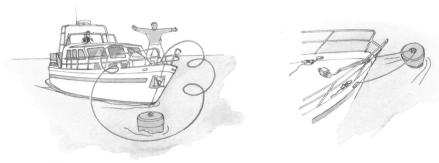

Stern pick-up

On some boats it is easier to pick the buoy up at the stern. This allows the crew easier access to the buoy and may give the helmsman better vision. Because the stern seeks the wind in reverse, this is easier than it looks. Ensure there are no lines on the buoy that could catch around the prop.

Lead a line from the bow, outside the rails, to the stern. Thread the line through the ring and walk it forward to the bow as the boat rotates head to wind.

Mooring to piles

Pile moorings consist of a pair of wooden or steel piles driven into the seabed, between which the boat is moored. The user end of a pile mooring is the riser bar and ring. The lines are attached to a ring that slides up and down the riser bar with the rise and fall of tide.

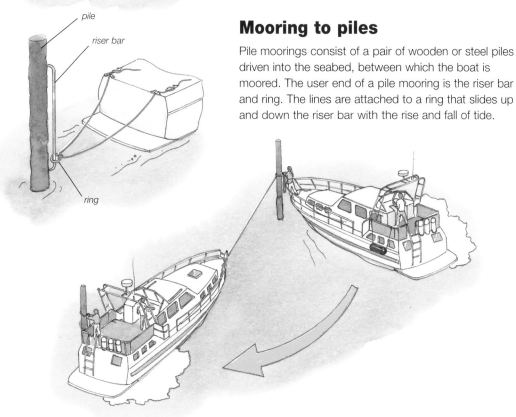

Connect a line to the upstream/wind pile mooring. If it is to tricky to pass a line through the ring, simply loop the bow line through the riser bar and bring it back on board.

Using a combination of stream, wind and outside engine, ease yourself back to the stern pile. The outside engine pivots the stern towards the aft pile. Attach two stern lines, one from either side, to the ring. If required, ease forward to the bow pile and re-secure. Ideally, two stern and two bow lines are used to keep the boat centred.

14 Safe speed

Think ahead – if you are travelling at 20 knots you need to be thinking at 30 knots. Only travel at the speed at which you can still make good decisions and safely control the boat.

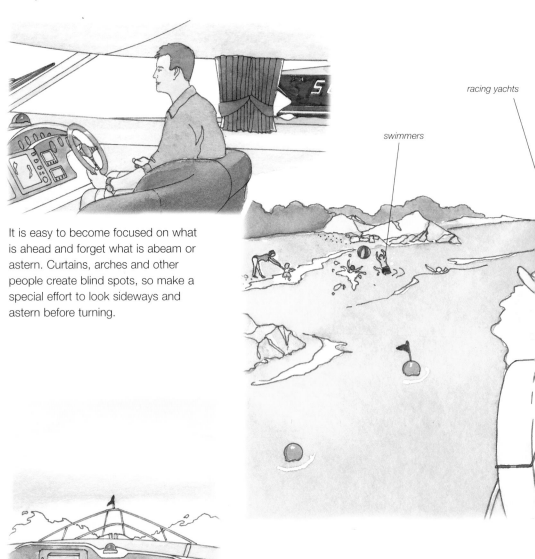

racing yachts

swimmers

It is easy to become focused on what is ahead and forget what is abeam or astern. Curtains, arches and other people create blind spots, so make a special effort to look sideways and astern before turning.

Adjust your speed to suit conditions. Fog and reduced visibility require slower speeds and extra care.

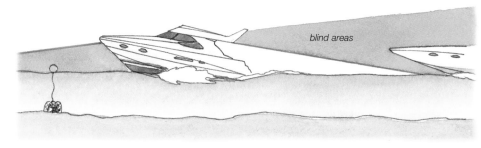

blind areas

Because of the angle of trim, your vision may be impaired both ahead and astern.

Beware of obstructions, such as fishing pots or small buoys, that may be lurking under the bow.

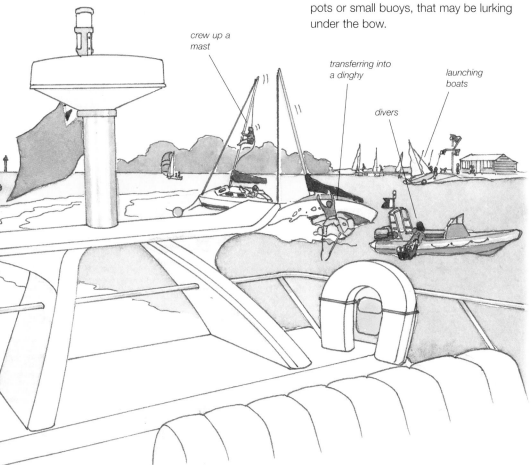

crew up a mast

transferring into a dinghy

launching boats

divers

There are a great many water users and all have a responsibility to each other. Motorboats can travel at high speeds and kick up a lot of wash that affects the safety and enjoyment of other water users. Be especially careful around harbours and mind your wash.

Sailing boats need to zigzag, so slow down and go behind them. Watch what they are doing and anticipate their manoeuvres. Be patient and clear in your intentions.

Divers can surface well away from their boat so use extreme vigilance.

Keep a good lookout at all times. If you are the give way vessel, make your intentions clear and in plenty of time, so that the other vessel knows exactly what you are doing.

Does a risk of collision exist?

Check whether the vessel is on a collision course in the following ways:

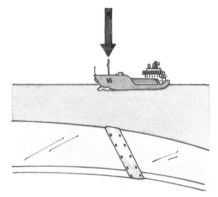

Line the vessel up on a part of the boat and keep a steady course. If it stays lined up, you'll collide.

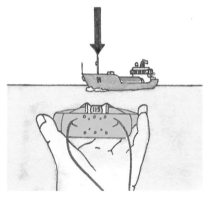

Whilst maintaining a steady course, look through either the ship's compass or a hand-held compass. If the bearing stays the same, you'll collide.

Radar

If the target stays on the same relative bearing, you will collide. Use the radar's electronic bearing line (EBL) to check whether another vessel is maintaining the same bearings.

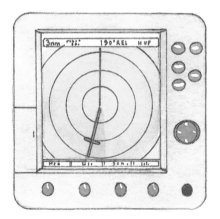

Top Tip

When giving way, either change course or slow down. When slowing down, the aspect of the boat initially stays the same, so slow in plenty of time to make your intention clear.

Narrow channels

Vessels constrained by their draught in narrow channels should not be impeded. They cannot alter course without the risk of grounding, so stay away.

- If possible, stay outside the main channel – look at the chart to check the water depth.

- If crossing a channel, cross at 90 degrees when it is clear to do so.

- Be especially aware in bad visibility, when it is easy to slip into the channel – the depth is a good indication of position. If crossing a channel in bad visibility, consider calling the port radio – they may be tracking all vessels on their radar and will advise.

- Even around shallow channels there may be enough water for you to stay outside the channel with sufficient rise of tide. Check the chart and tidal information.

- Look at the chart to see if local regulations are in force governing the use of channels.

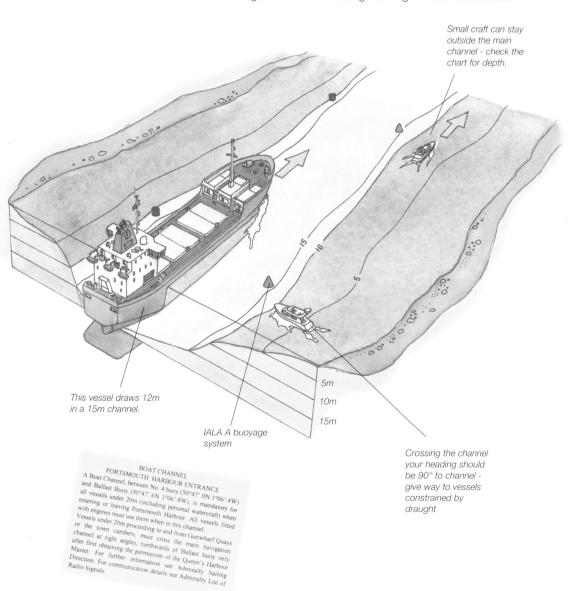

Small craft can stay outside the main channel - check the chart for depth.

This vessel draws 12m in a 15m channel.

5m

10m

15m

IALA A buoyage system

Crossing the channel your heading should be 90° to channel - give way to vessels constrained by draught

BOAT CHANNEL
PORTSMOUTH HARBOUR ENTRANCE
A Boat Channel, between No. 4 buoy (50°47'.0N 1°06'.4W) and Ballast Buoy (50°47'.6N 1°06'.8W), is mandatory for all vessels under 20m (including personal watercraft) when entering or leaving Portsmouth Harbour. All vessels fitted with engines must use them when in this channel. Vessels under 20m proceeding to and from Gunwharf Quays or the town cambers, must cross the main navigation channel at right angles, northwards of Ballast buoy only after first obtaining the permission of the Queen's Harbour Master. For further information see Admiralty Sailing Direction. For communication details see Admiralty List of Radio Signals.

16 Cruising at speed

Cruisers get from A to B very quickly, but also use a lot of fuel doing so. Fuel consumption is extremely important because there are no fuel stations along the way and fuelling en route usually entails a lengthy detour into port.

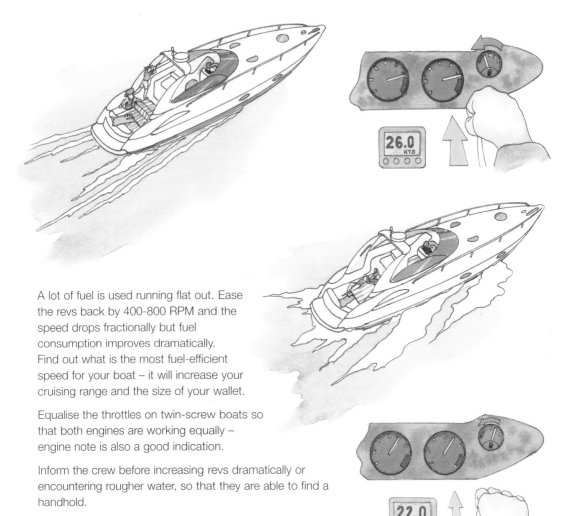

A lot of fuel is used running flat out. Ease the revs back by 400-800 RPM and the speed drops fractionally but fuel consumption improves dramatically. Find out what is the most fuel-efficient speed for your boat – it will increase your cruising range and the size of your wallet.

Equalise the throttles on twin-screw boats so that both engines are working equally – engine note is also a good indication.

Inform the crew before increasing revs dramatically or encountering rougher water, so that they are able to find a handhold.

Maximum loading

If the boat is loaded with the maximum amount of people, its characteristics change drastically. Firstly, it will use more fuel – up to 20% more – and it will take longer to get up onto the plane or cruising speed.

If you are planning a passage, allow at least a 20% margin of reserve fuel. If you are using too much fuel, slow down. Weather and sea state have a dramatic effect on speed, so look for flat water and shelter.

Trim under power 17

Trim is the fore and aft attitude of the boat. Raising or lowering the stern changes the strike area of the hull hitting the waves and is adjusted by moving the trim tabs up or down or an outdrive leg in or out. It affects comfort, fuel consumption and the handling characteristics, especially in heavy weather.

Power trim

An outdrive leg is trimmed in or out to change the angle of the propeller's thrust. Trim affects comfort, fuel consumption and the handling characteristics, especially in heavy weather.

Leg in to start – to keep the prop in the water and help the boat get on the plane.

On the plane, ease the leg out to achieve the best speed. Adjusted by the correct amount the revs increase slightly without the throttle being adjusted, therefore speed increases.

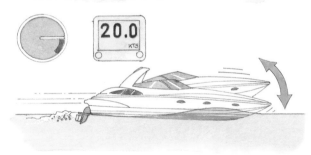

Ease out too much and the prop sucks in air from the surface, making it spin faster but lose grip on the water, slowing the boat. If the boat starts to porpoise, trim the leg-in to regain control, and then slowly ease out to re-trim.

Trim needs constant adjustment. If crew move around the boat or there is a change in sea conditions or speed, you need to check on trim to maintain the best fuel consumption. Fuel use makes the boat lighter – you will need to trim between full and half tanks.

Watching the difference between engine revs and speed is a good indication of correct trim.

Legs can be helpful getting up on the plane. They should not be needed, but may compensate for the crew standing at the rear or a weedy hull.

Trim tabs

Trim tabs are electrical or hydraulically operated flaps fitted either side on the stern. They are used together or independently to alter the fore and aft trim and heeling of the boat. They work by deflecting water flow, and the faster the boat is travelling, the greater the effect.

One tab down – raises one side of the boat. This is useful to compensate for loading irregularities, a beam sea or a strong crosswind.

Tabs down – lowers the bow and raises the stern.

Gauges are seldom fitted to inform you how much trim is used. While in port count how long the tabs take to rise, lower and centre, then use time increments for their positioning.

Tabs up – raises the bow and lowers the stern.

Although tabs are mainly used at speed, they can also be used tabbed down in marinas to increase grip on the water. Beware of powerful reversing when tabbed down, as this can cause them damage.

Tabs make a huge difference to comfort and sea-keeping ability at speed. It is even possible to achieve basic steering using one tab at a time when at speed. Experimentation in different conditions will give the best compromise of comfort, fuel consumption and ride, but two thirds down is a reasonable starting point.

Trim in large waves

Head sea

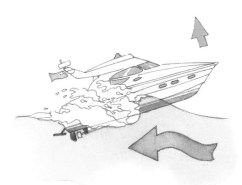

In a head sea, tab down, so that the forward vee sections cut into and through the waves. This ensures maximum length of hull in the water to reduce slamming.

If tabbed up, the bow is continually thrown into the air, creating lots of spray and increasing slamming.

Outdrives also require the leg-in to push the bow down and to keep the prop in the water.

Following sea

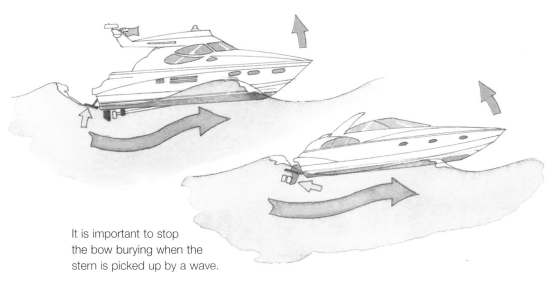

It is important to stop the bow burying when the stern is picked up by a wave.

Trim the tabs up so that the bow is up, and adjust your speed to be slower or faster than the wave.

Outdrive boats may need the leg trimming out to raise the bow.

Large wave tactics

Damage is easily caused by driving straight into a wave. It puts a colossal load on the structure of the boat as it slams into the wave and crashes through the other side.

Pick your way through the sea by choosing a zigzag course. This gives more time to reach the next wave, as the crests will be further apart. Reduce speed to stop slamming, although you should be wary of slowing too much as you may loose all directional stability – a compromise speed should be found.

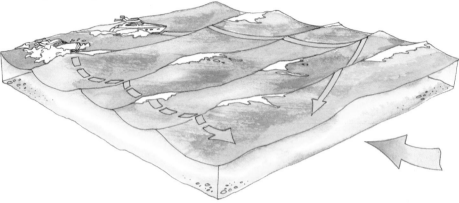

Large wave dangers

Broaching

Broaching happens when a wave crest picks up the stern (a), causing the bow to dig in (b) and the boat to slew beam onto the sea and get rolled over (c). Adjust your speed downwind so that you are either faster or slower than the wave crest. In heavy weather you may need to tow long warps or a drogue to stop the stern from being picked up and thrown about. Breaking crests on the beam are dangerous and should be avoided by steering down or upwind instead.

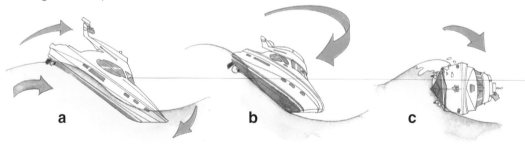

a   b   c

Damage control

If a window or port-light gets smashed, turn that side of the boat away from the oncoming sea. Block the hole with bunk cushions or doors to reduce water ingress. If one window has failed it is probable that the others will follow, so consider running downwind if sea room permits. Contact the Coastguard and keep them informed of your progress.

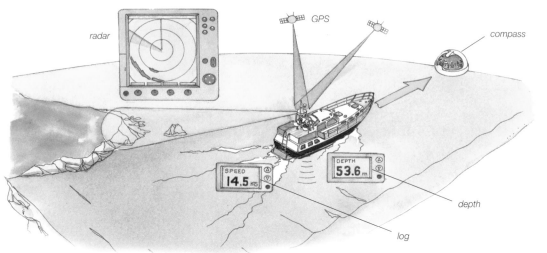

radar

GPS

compass

SPEED
14.5 KTS

DEPTH
53.6 m

depth

log

Radar	uses microwaves to reflect off objects at sea. Reflections are displayed on a screen.
GPS	Global Positioning System, uses satellites to give a position. The position is displayed as co-ordinates or on electronic chart screen.
Log	reads speed and distance through the water from a paddlewheel or ultrasonic water sensor fitted through the hull.
Depth	calculates depth of water by a sound-wave transducer fitted through the hull.
Compass	magnetic compass for steering direction.
Autopilot	hydraulically or electrically operated automatic steering system that can be interfaced with other instruments, such as GPS (to steer to a waypoint).
Fluxgate compass	electronic compass allowing interfacing with autopilot (for steering) and radar (for collision avoidance). Highly sensitive gyro-rate compasses are becoming more common on autopilots to give improved accuracy for automatic radar collision-alerting systems (MARPA).
Interfacing	allows two or more instruments to talk to each other and share information. Usually interfacing is as simple as connecting two wires together. Interfacing between GPS and autopilot allows the boat to steer to a waypoint automatically.
VHF/DSC Radio	very high frequency radio for communication with other vessels, marinas, ports and coastguard. DSC radios interfaced to GPS send out vessels position in an emergency

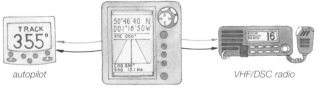

TRACK
355°

50°46'40 N
001°18'50 W
XTE 000°

COG 330°
SOG 13.1 kts

16

autopilot

VHF/DSC radio

GPS

GPS

GPS (Global Positioning System) is a satellite-fixing system run and maintained by the USA and gives accuracy to 10-20 metres. It consists of 24-30 satellites orbiting the Earth, of which four are required at any one time to give a fix. GPS sets used onboard usually pick up 6-12 satellites for better accuracy and less chance of spurious data. Position can be viewed in the form of map co-ordinates, latitude and longitude, or on an electronic chart portrayed on a chartplotter or onboard computer screen.

GPS jargon

Position – given in latitude and longitude.

Waypoint – User defined point on chart to which the GPS will give a distance and bearing to steer.

COG – course over ground.

Because your position is continually updated, the GPS calculates the course over the ground you are achieving.

SOG – speed over ground.
Calculates your speed over ground, taking stream and drift into account.

BTW – bearing to waypoint.
Gives precise bearing to a user-defined point on chart.

DTW – distance to waypoint.

XTE – cross-track error.
Shows how far off track you are on your journey to a waypoint.

ETA – estimated time of arrival at waypoint.

Accuracy

GPS works by comparing timing signals from GPS satellites. The difference in time is small and is calculated using highly accurate atomic clocks. However, the time signals can suffer delays as they pass through the ionosphere causing inaccuracies.

SDGPS

Satellite Differential GPS calculates the idiosyncrasies of delay through the Ionosphere. It looks at where the GPS position thinks it is, compares it with its actual position, and plots the difference. It improves accuracy to about 5 metres, but more importantly, improves the integrity of the signal. If you are buying a GPS set look for one that is capable of receiving SDGPS. The Common SDGPS systems operated worldwide are: WAAS (Wide Area Augmentation System) in the USA; and EGNOS (European Geostationary Navigational Overlay System) in Europe; and in Asia; MSAS (Japanese Multi-Functional Satellite Augmentation System). Buying a GPS receiver that is WAAS, EGNOS or MSAS ready, will receive the SDGPS signals.

GPS use

Horizontal Datum

Satellite-derived positions are usually referred to a WGS 84 datum. Charts are referenced to many other types of datum, depending on the original survey on which they were based.

Find out the datum of the chart and select this datum in the GPS setup menu to reduce any possible errors. Differences between datums can be over 200 metres.

Waypoints

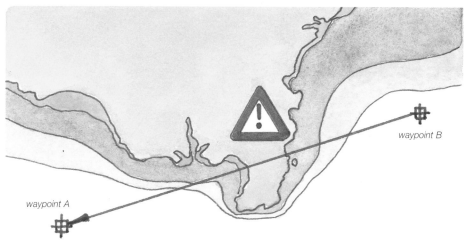

waypoint B

waypoint A

Because GPS gives our position on the surface it can calculate our course to another position decided by the user. These user-defined points are called waypoints and can be placed anywhere we choose.

The A-to-B course given by a GPS will be the most direct route and could be straight through a landmass. It is sometimes better to follow a route of waypoints placed along the way. Always double check waypoint co-ordinates by plotting them onto the chart, then comparing the GPS data with the actual course and distance.

Log it

Always keep a record of your GPS position on the chart or in a logbook so that if the GPS fails, there is a last-known position from which to work.

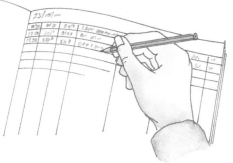

Plotters and PCs

A graphical portrayal of position is more understandable than a series of numbers quoted in Latitude and Longitude. Graphical portrayal of position is possible on electronic charts displayed on a chartplotter or a computer with navigational software installed.

Chart plotters

Chart plotters are dedicated stand-alone display units that have a GPS receiver built-in. They tend to be built ruggedly, most are waterproof for exterior mounting, and they do not to mind being jolted about because they are designed for the job. The software is controlled using a few buttons and the operating logic is menu driven. However just as a mobile phone, if you are not familiar with the operation, it may take practice to become confident with its use.

PC software

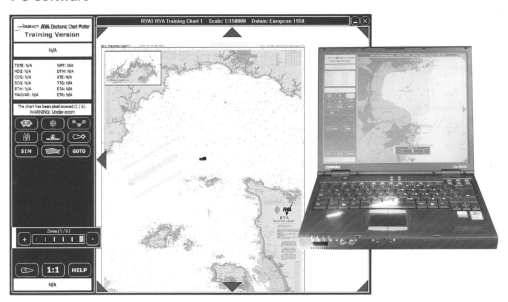

Computers on boats come in three forms; laptops are the most common, followed by PDA (Personal Desktop Assistants) and then purpose built marine PCs. As the cost of PCs and flat screen technology reduces, built in systems will become the norm. Computers are loaded with a chart software navigation program, using a CD that will run electronic charts. The PC needs to be interfaced with a GPS unit so that the vessels position can be displayed on the screen. Most PCs require a voltage change through either a transformer or inverter unless they are purpose built.

Radar

Radar works by sending out radio waves that rebound of a solid object, back to the radar. These radio echoes are then displayed on a screen. The size and strength of the echo depend on what's reflected. A tanker will give a better echo than a small wooden sailing boat.

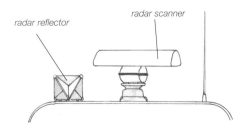

radar reflector   radar scanner

To increase a small boat's echo, radar reflectors are placed on the fly bridge or deck head to amplify the signal return. Even if radar is fitted, a reflector is still required by law (see reference section SOLAS V).

Radar can interface with most marine electronics. If interfaced with a very good electronic compass it can work MARPA Mini Assisted Radar Plotting Aids, which can identify and warn you of possible collisions.

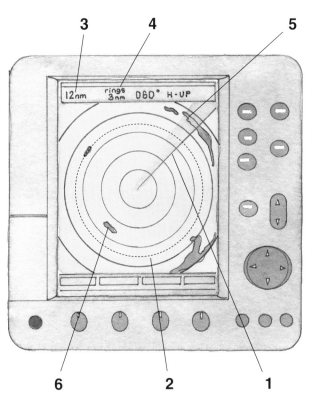

Radar jargon

1 **EBL** – Electronic Bearing Line – allows bearings to be taken of echoes.

2 **VRM** – Variable Range Marker – allows distance to be taken from echoes.

3 **Range** – different ranges can be selected depending on area of use (12 miles offshore $1/4$ mile when entering a harbour).

4 **Range rings** – these change depending on range selected, and give useful reference for distance off.

5 **Radar fix** – distance off from VRM and bearing from EBL of well-defined point gives a fix.

6 **Target** – vessel or object on radar screen. If it keeps a constant bearing it will collide.

Radar is a complex subject. Enrol on an RYA Radar course or read the RYA Radar book. Also practice using radar in good weather first.

Chart basics

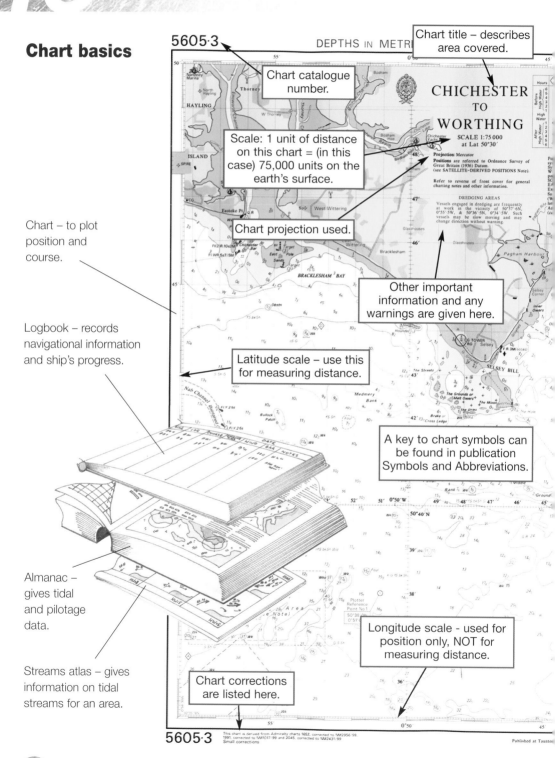

5605·3

DEPTHS IN METR...

Chart title – describes area covered.

Chart catalogue number.

Scale: 1 unit of distance on this chart = (in this case) 75,000 units on the earth's surface.

Chart projection used.

Chart – to plot position and course.

Logbook – records navigational information and ship's progress.

Other important information and any warnings are given here.

Latitude scale – use this for measuring distance.

A key to chart symbols can be found in publication Symbols and Abbreviations.

Almanac – gives tidal and pilotage data.

Longitude scale - used for position only, NOT for measuring distance.

Streams atlas – gives information on tidal streams for an area.

Chart corrections are listed here.

5605·3

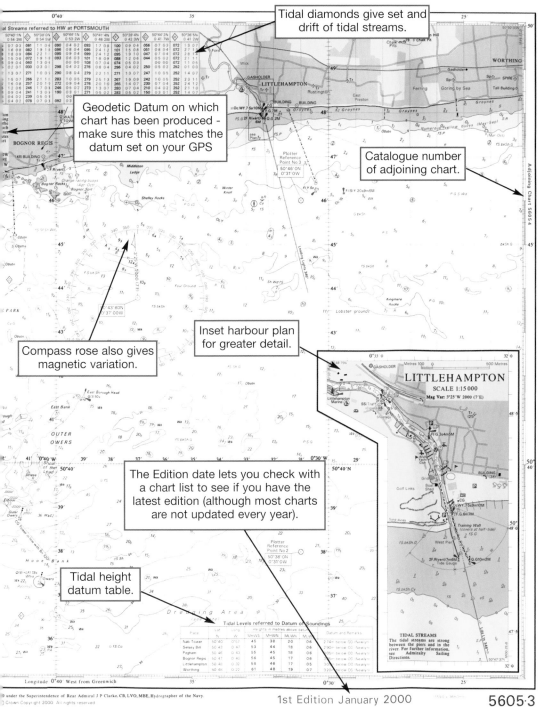

Tidal diamonds give set and drift of tidal streams.

Geodetic Datum on which chart has been produced - make sure this matches the datum set on your GPS

Catalogue number of adjoining chart.

Compass rose also gives magnetic variation.

Inset harbour plan for greater detail.

The Edition date lets you check with a chart list to see if you have the latest edition (although most charts are not updated every year).

Tidal height datum table.

LITTLEHAMPTON
SCALE 1:15 000
Mag Var: 3°25'W 2000 (7°E)

TIDAL STREAMS
The tidal streams are strong between the piers and in the river. For further information, see Admiralty Sailing Directions.

1st Edition January 2000

5605·3

Navigation Basics - Compass errors

Deviation

This occurs when ferrous objects close to a compass create errors. Each compass should have a deviation card that gives the error on each heading. Do not place or sight electronics or metal objects close to a compass. Compass adjusters will correct your compass or make up a card for you; so that you can calculate the deviation on different headings.

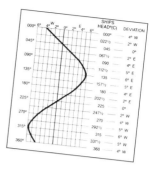

SHIPS HEAD°(C)	DEVIATION
000°	4° W
022½	2° W
045	0°
067½	2° E
090	4° E
112½	5° E
135	6° E
157½	5° E
180	4° E
202½	2° E
225	0°
247½	2° W
270	4° W
292½	5° W
315	6° W
337½	5° W
360	4° W

Variation

magnetic north *true north*

All compasses point to magnetic north. Charts show north as true north. The difference between true and magnetic north is called variation.

Variation changes according to position. Variation in your area is shown on the compass rose and marked in pencil on your plotter.

Mark off variation on plotter

Plotting a course

A Plotter is used to establish direction once it is referenced to North on the chart.

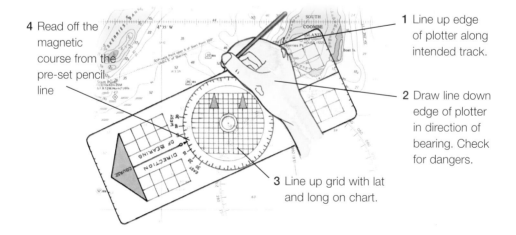

4 Read off the magnetic course from the pre-set pencil line

1 Line up edge of plotter along intended track.

2 Draw line down edge of plotter in direction of bearing. Check for dangers.

3 Line up grid with lat and long on chart.

Measuring distance

Dividers are used to measure distance from the side of the chart.

To find the distance of your route.

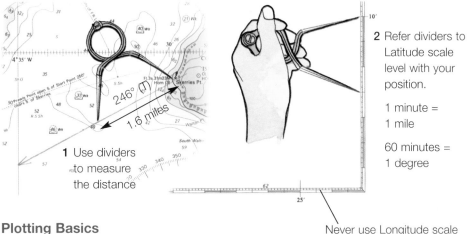

1 Use dividers to measure the distance

2 Refer dividers to Latitude scale level with your position.

1 minute = 1 mile

60 minutes = 1 degree

Never use Longitude scale to measure distance.

Plotting Basics

1 Dead reckoning

A basic position is gained by plotting course steered and distance travelled.

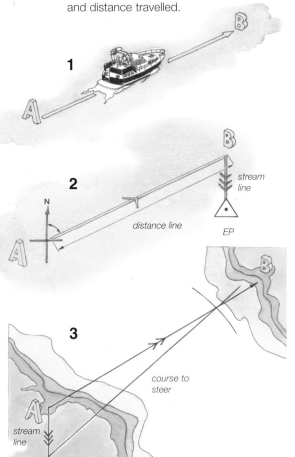

2 Estimated position

A better estimate of your position is possible if you have; kept a log of your speed, direction, and calculated the stream.

To plot a current EP:

1 Plot course steered.

2 Measure off the distance travelled.

3 Add stream direction and distance on the end of distance line.

The end of the stream line is your EP (estimated position).

3 Course to steer

To work out a course to steer requires:

A starting point. Estimated speed. Length of passage. Stream direction and speed.

- A to B is 15 miles.
- We are travelling at 15 knots.
- It will take an hour.
- Plot A-to-B line.
- From A, plot 1 hour stream direction and rate.
- From end of stream line, measure off 15 miles until it crosses A-to-B line.

This is the CTS.

Tide basics

Tides occur because of the gravitational pull of the moon and sun affecting our seas. There are two HWs (High Waters) per day as the Earth rotates. Each cycle between LW (Low Water) and HW takes approximately 6 hours.

Spring tides

When moon and sun are working in parallel, the gravitational pull is greater, giving larger movements of water. These are Spring tides. The maximum difference (range) between the LW and HW height will be greater.

Neap tides

When the sun and moon are working at right angles to each other, the gravitational pull is lessened, and Neap tides are the result. The maximum difference (range) between LW and HW height will be smaller.

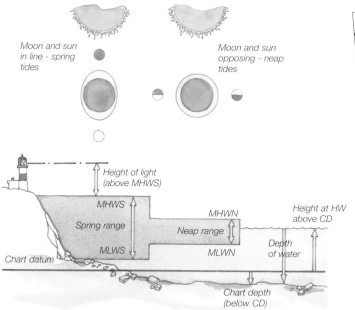

We get tidal information from an Almanac or tide tables. Remember to add or subtract hours in different countries or time zones.

Factors effecting height

Barometric pressure alters the height of water. The standard reference pressure is 1013mb but it is rounded down to 1010mb for these calculations. A change of 10mb changes the water height by 0.1m. High pressure at 1040mb reduces the water height by 0.3m.

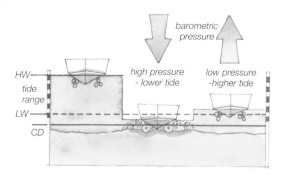

Top Tip

Ensure there is enough water below the propellers. Remember that the stern digs in and draws more when underway.

Streams and currents

Streams act like a conveyor belt. Get on a belt going the right way and you'll get to your destination quickly. A belt going the opposite way means you will take a lot longer or that you need to run to get there in the same amount of time.

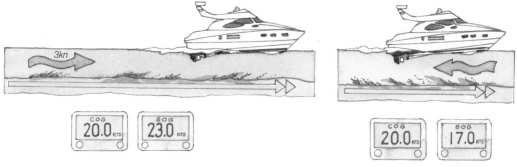

Going with the stream

The speed through the water, shown on the log is 20 knots, but the SOG (speed over ground) increases to include the three-knot stream. Instead of travelling 20 miles in one hour, you actually travel 23 miles. However, the log will read 20 miles distance travelled, as this is the amount of water through which you have travelled.

Going against the stream

The speed through the water, 20 knots on the log, stays the same but the SOG decreases. Instead of travelling 20 miles in one hour, you actually only manages 17 miles. The log will still read 20 miles travelled.

Streams affecting course

Streams coming from ahead or astern only affect our speed over ground. Streams coming from the side affect our direction and course over ground.

1 Even though the boat is steering a compass course for point B, it will end up at point C because the cross stream is affecting its course over ground.

2 To reach B, the boat should point into the stream to allow for the stream pushing it sideways. By calculating where the boat needs to be pointing to compensate for the cross stream, a course to steer is required (see below).

The strength and direction of the stream is found using a tidal atlas or almanac, or by a tidal diamond on a chart.

20 Passage planning

Pre-plan the passage

The following passage is based on the ficticional RYA Training Chart 1 and is not to be used for navigation.

How far is it and how long will it take – do we have sufficient fuel?

What are the passage constraints?

Pilotage – will it be day or night?

Boltholes – where to go if the weather turns or a boat problem arises?

Weather – shall we go? Motorboats are faster in a flat sea.

Navigation - work out a course to steer.

1 On a passage from Plymouth to St Helier Jersey work out the distance = 66M. At 15 knots cruising the passage would take about 4$\frac{1}{2}$ hours.

Constraints

Look in the Pilot Book and Almanac to find out what constraints there are to the passage.

2 St Helier has a sill that only allows access ±3 hours HW Our arrival time is dictated by this.

3 Our next constraint is the Alderney race this has very fast tides.

Use a tidal atlas to determine the tide on the passage. Ensure you pass through the race with the wind and tide together.

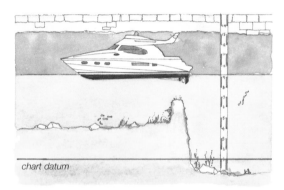
chart datum

St Helier marina, access HW±3 over sill (CD+3.6m);

6 hours after HW Plymouth (1 hour after HW Dover)

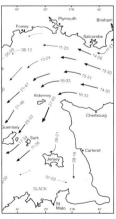

5 hours before HW Plymouth (2 hours after HW Dover)

4 hours before HW Plymouth (3 hours after HW Dover)

3 hours before HW Plymouth (4 hours after HW Dover)

Pilotage for Jersey

4 Plan your pilotage before you leave. It is
a lot easier whilst alongside than at 15
knots. Simplify the chart to the main
points required for entry.

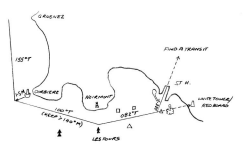

Plan the route

5 Plymouth to the Alderney Race is across
the stream and will need a course to
steer. Once through the Alderney Race,
the tide is pushing towards Jersey so a
direct course can be plotted.

Plymouth to Alderney Race is 30 miles
and takes 2 hours. Use 2 hours of tide to
construct the course to steer.

Add Waypoints.

6 Draw waypoints (WPs) onto chart, and
mark down the
Lat and Long.
Enter WPs into
GPS. Double-
check the WPs
by comparing
bearings and
distances to
WPs with those
from the chart.

Boltholes

7 Identify places to which you could run in
foul weather or if you encountered engine
problems.

Cherbourg or Alderney offer shelter
except from the north. Sark offers
anchorages on each of its four sides.

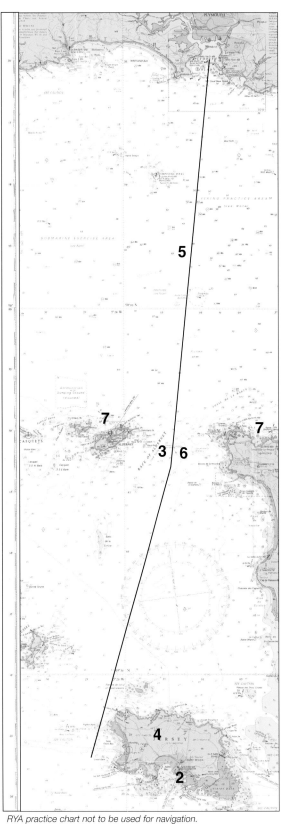

RYA practice chart not to be used for navigation.

The Passage

Weather

Keep an eye on the weather to build up a picture of what is happening. Get the latest forecasts and ensure the weather window will stay good long enough for a longer than normal passage. If in doubt don't go.

A fast and comfortable passage is possible in smooth conditions but rougher seas can reduce you to displacement speed taking twice as long.

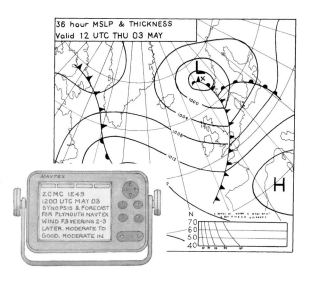

Navigation

1 Check the boats position on GPS as you pass a known point. This ensures that the GPS is set up correctly with the chart.

Waypoints

If your course is across the tide do not steer for waypoint, stay on your course to steer and the stream will edge you across.

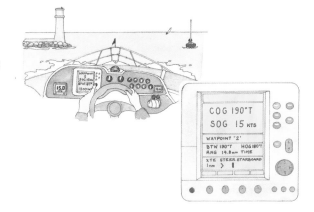

Radar

2 Radar can be used to give a distance and bearing. Here the Eddystone Lighthouse is on starboard beam at 3.8 miles.

Remember most radars portray a picture relative to your heading.

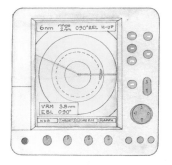

Lookout

3 Entering shipping lanes. Keep good lookout. Here the ships initially come from the east then from the west In shipping lanes for the next 40 minutes.

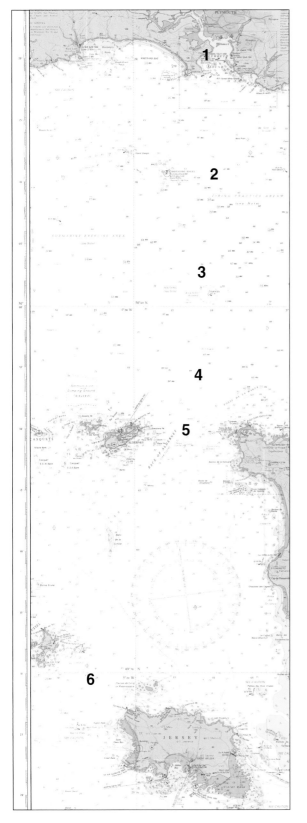

Keep a log

4 Plot position in logbook or on chart at 30 minute intervals. If your electronics fail you have a record from which a position can be derived on a paper chart and a new course plotted.

Radar lookout

5 Radar clearly shows, abeam, Alderney on starboard 2.8M and Cap de la Hague on Port 5.7M.

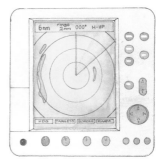

Transits

6 Transits will give an accurate line of position. Pt Robert and Blanchard E Cardinal in transit.

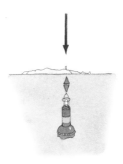

Running the pilotage

When piloting, always know exactly where you are. If in doubt stop, go back to a known point and start again. In open water, 15 knots may seem slow, but in a pilotage situation it is very fast indeed. Reduce speed down to 5-6 knots then slow some more as required. Remember: only travel as fast as you can compute the information and make the correct calls.

Waypoint web

1 Consider drawing a waypoint web to give bearing and distance from a WP. Useful for quick plotting of position or when needed quickly.

Depth

2 Changes in depth give good indication of position.

Plotters

3 A chart plotter gives a quick visual check on your position.

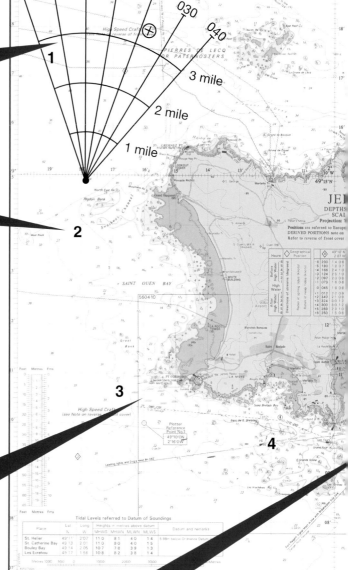

Compass check

4 When steering a compass course towards a point; if the compass heading changes you are drifting.

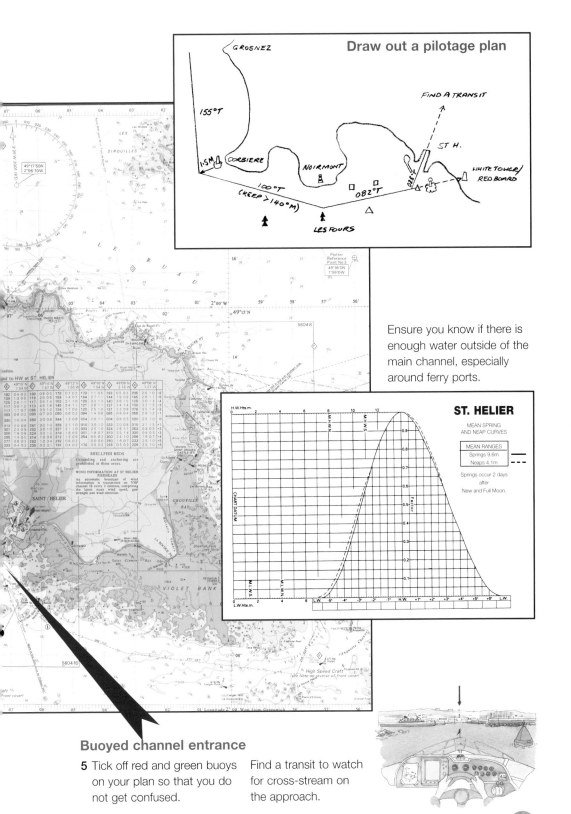

Draw out a pilotage plan

GROSNEZ

155°T

1·5M CORBIERE

NOIRMONT

100°T
(KEEP >140°M)

082°T

LES FOURS

ST H.

OLD.

FIND A TRANSIT

WHITE TOWER/
RED BOARD

49°17'50N
2°06'70W

49°12'N
1·56 W

49°10 N
1·56 W

49'09 N
2·19 W

49°08 N
1·67 W

HW.Hts.m.

Ensure you know if there is
enough water outside of the
main channel, especially
around ferry ports.

ST. HELIER

MEAN SPRING
AND NEAP CURVES

MEAN RANGES
Springs 9.6m
Neaps 4.1m

Springs occur 2 days
after
New and Full Moon.

CHART DATUM

L.W.Hts.m.

M.L.W.S.
M.L.W.N.

M.H.W.N.
M.H.W.S.

L.W. -5° -4° -3° -2° -1° H.W. +1° +2° +3° +4° +5° +6° L.W.

Factor

Buoyed channel entrance

5 Tick off red and green buoys
on your plan so that you do
not get confused.

Find a transit to watch
for cross-stream on
the approach.

21 Weather

General overview

Low and high-pressure systems dictate our weather. They revolve in different directions, depending on which hemisphere they inhabit. Where you are cruising on the earth's surface will dictate whether lows, highs or a mixture of both dictate your weather. In the UK, low-pressure systems dictate our weather. In many places in the Southern hemisphere cold fronts dictate the weather scene.

In the Northern Hemisphere Low pressure systems revolve anticlockwise and Highs revolve clockwise

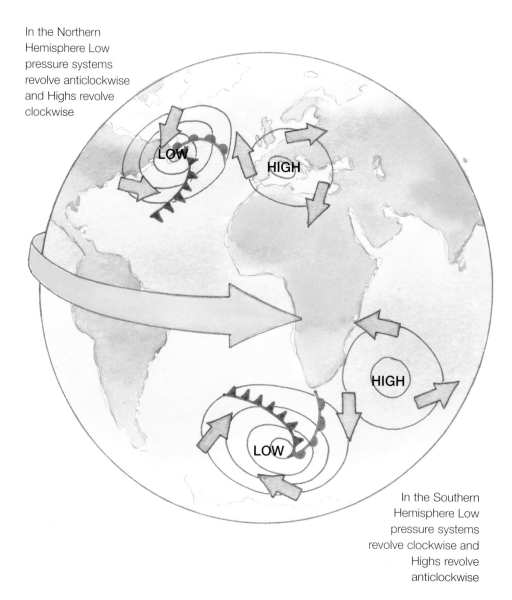

In the Southern Hemisphere Low pressure systems revolve clockwise and Highs revolve anticlockwise

Northern hemisphere

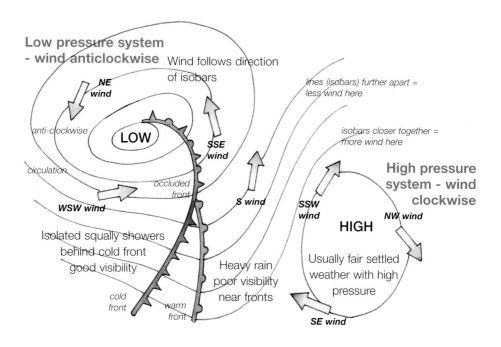

Low pressure system - wind anticlockwise

Wind follows direction of isobars

NE wind

lines (isobars) further apart = less wind here

anti-clockwise

LOW

SSE wind

isobars closer together = more wind here

circulation

occluded front

S wind

SSW wind

NW wind

WSW wind

High pressure system - wind clockwise

HIGH

Isolated squally showers behind cold front good visibility

Usually fair settled weather with high pressure

cold front

warm front

Heavy rain poor visibility near fronts

SE wind

Southern hemisphere

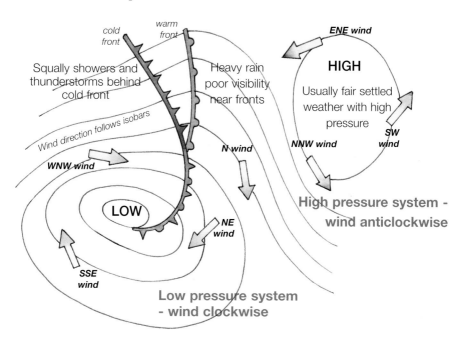

cold front

warm front

ENE wind

Squally showers and thunderstorms behind cold front

Heavy rain poor visibility near fronts

HIGH

Usually fair settled weather with high pressure

Wind direction follows isobars

WNW wind

N wind

NNW wind

SW wind

LOW

NE wind

High pressure system - wind anticlockwise

SSE wind

Low pressure system - wind clockwise

Terms used in forecasts

Gale warnings	If average wind is expected to be F8 or more, or gusts 43-51kn.
Strong wind	If average wind is expected to be F6 or F7.
Warnings	F6 is often called a 'yachtsman's gale'.
Imminent	Within 6 hrs of time of issue of warning.
Soon	Within 6-12 hrs of time of issue of warning.
Later	More than 12 hrs from time of issue of warning.
Visibility	*Good* - greater than 5 miles *Moderate* - between 2 - 5 miles. *Poor* - 1,000m to 2 miles. Fog less than 1,000m.
Fair	No significant precipitation.
Backing	Wind changing in an anticlockwise direction eg NW to SW.
Veering	Wind changing in a clockwise direction eg NE to SE.
General synopsis	How and where the weather systems are moving.
Sea states	*Smooth* - wave height 0.2 - 0.5m *Slight* - wave height 0.5 - 1.25m. *Moderate* - wave height 1.25 - 2.5m *Rough* - wave height 2.5 - 4m. *Very rough* - wave height 4 - 6m.

Land and sea breezes

Sea breeze

Land breeze

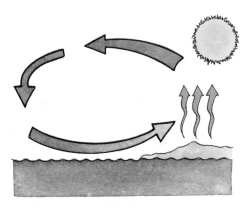

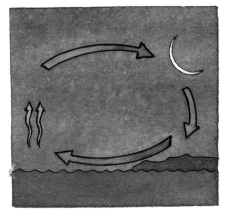

In fair weather and light to moderate offshore wind, a sea breeze is likely to develop. Warm air rises over land, it then cools, descends and blows onshore. Wind up to force 4 in strength.

This occurs on a clear night when the air cools over land and flows downhill and out to sea, particularly from river estuaries.

Wind usually no more than force 2- 3 except near mountains.

Beaufort wind force

Force 1-3 (1-10 knots)

Perfect motor cruising. Fast-planing conditions. Occasional wave crests.

Force 3-5 (7-21 knots)

Boisterous seas at the top of the Force range when sheltered water should be found. May need to slow down in larger seas.

Force 6 and above (21 knots and above)

Large waves, white foam crests. Displacement speed. Glad to see port.

It is not only high winds that create large and dangerous seas. Very rough water develops all around the coastline depending on wind direction and the direction of the current.

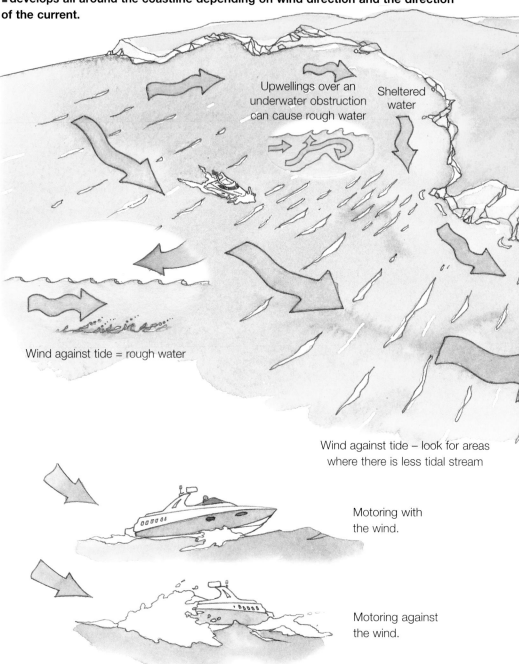

Upwellings over an underwater obstruction can cause rough water

Sheltered water

Wind against tide = rough water

Wind against tide – look for areas where there is less tidal stream

Motoring with the wind.

Motoring against the wind.

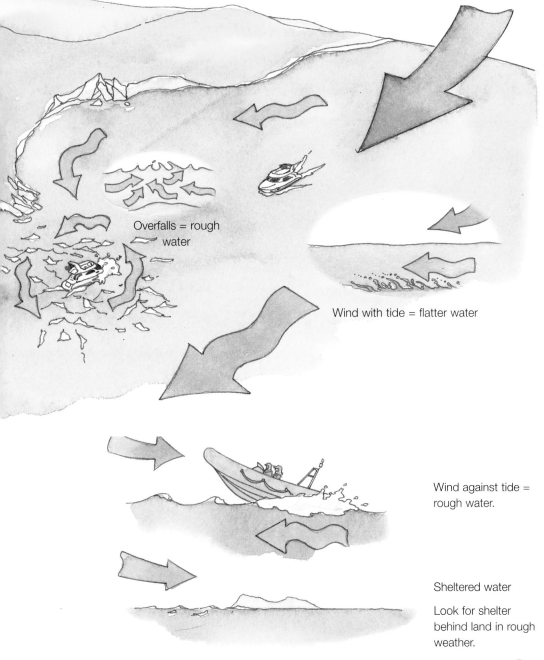

Overfalls = rough
water

Wind with tide = flatter water

Wind against tide =
rough water.

Sheltered water

Look for shelter
behind land in rough
weather.

Navigation lights

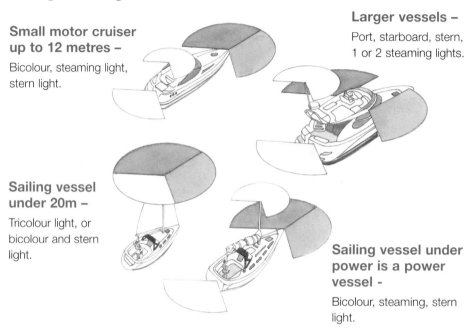

Small motor cruiser up to 12 metres –

Bicolour, steaming light, stern light.

Larger vessels –

Port, starboard, stern, 1 or 2 steaming lights.

Sailing vessel under 20m –

Tricolour light, or bicolour and stern light.

Sailing vessel under power is a power vessel -

Bicolour, steaming, stern light.

Sound signals and priorities

In fog

Power driven vessel, making way ▬

Vessel under sail, making way ▬ • •

In sight of each other

I'm turning to port • •

I'm turning to starboard •

What are your intentions? You're not taking enough avoiding action.

My engines are running astern • • •

Priorities

Because motor vessels are extremely manoeuvrable, they give way to most other water users.

The order of priority when giving way is:

- Vessels not under command.
- Vessels constrained by draught or restricted in their ability to manoeuvre.
- Fishing boats or trawlers.
- Sailing boats.
- Motorboats.

Lights and shapes

Larger ships (over 50m) must have two masthead lights.

Starboard view

225°

225°

135°

112.5°

112.5°

From astern

From ahead

Port view

by day

At anchor

by day

Restricted in ability to manoeuvre

eg. dredging cable laying etc

by day

Carrying out underwater work

eg. large container ships or tankers in a narrow channel

3 all round reds

by day

Constrained by draught

by day

BF3

Fishing trawling

Other types of fishing

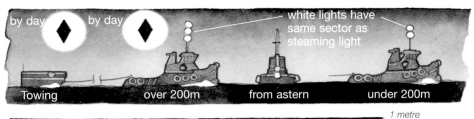

by day

by day

white lights have same sector as steaming light

Towing   over 200m   from astern   under 200m

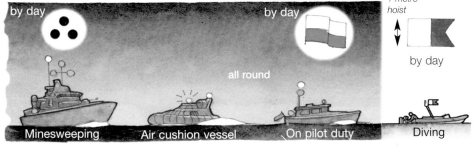

by day

by day

all round

1 metre hoist

by day

Minesweeping   **Air cushion vessel**   **On pilot duty**   **Diving**

24 Rules of the road

Who gives way

Crossing

Give way to vessels approaching from starboard. Vessel (A) gives way to vessel (B).

Head on

Both vessels turn to starboard. Pass port to port.

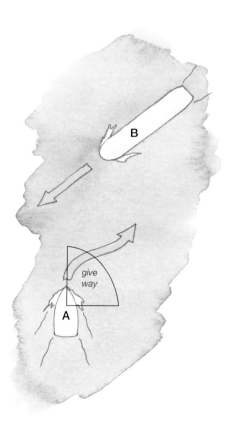

B

give
way

A

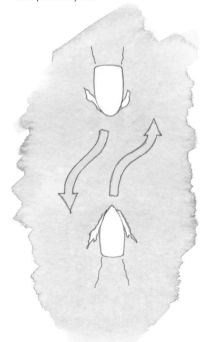

Overtaking vessel

Overtaking vessel keeps clear. The stand-on vessel should keep a steady course and speed.

Any vessel in the overtaking sector must give way to the stand-on vessel.

Motor on sail

Power gives way to sailing boats. Pass astern of sailing boats and keep wash to a minimum. Make your intentions clear early on.

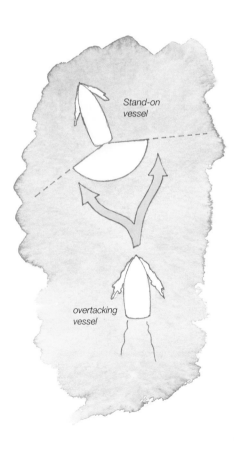

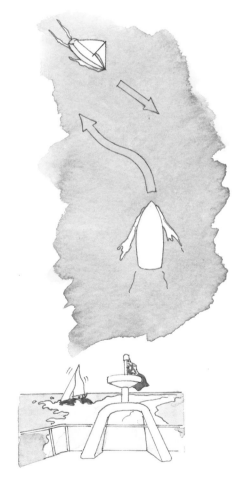

Keep wash to a minimum when passing close to yachts.

25 Buoyage & separation

Two buoyage systems exist in the world, IALA A and IALA B. The difference affects the colour and light characteristics of lateral marks.

IALA A is used in Europe, Africa, Russia, India, Australia and New Zealand.

IALA B, which is illustrated on page 60, is used in the USA, South America and parts of the Caribbean, South East Asia and Canada.

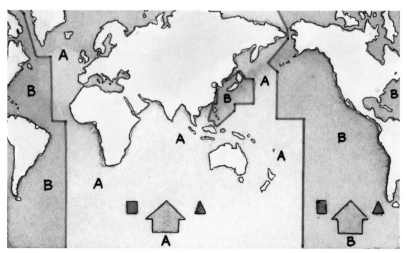

Cardinals

Cardinal marks warn of danger. and remain constant thouighout the IALA system.

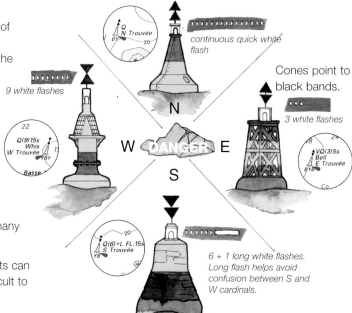

continuous quick white flash

9 white flashes

Cones point to black bands.

3 white flashes

6 + 1 long white flashes. Long flash helps avoid confusion between S and W cardinals.

Buoys are found in many shapes and sizes.

Solar panels and lights can make top marks difficult to distinguish.

Weed and guano can alter the appearance and colour.

OK

IALA - A Buoyage

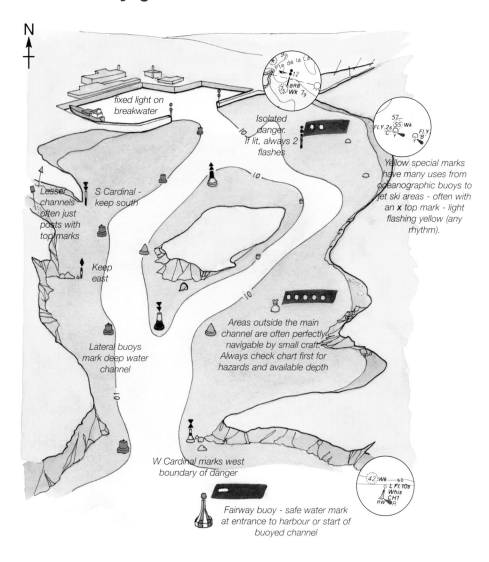

N

fixed light on breakwater

Isolated danger. If lit, always 2 flashes

Yellow special marks have many uses from oceanographic buoys to jet ski areas - often with an **x** top mark - light flashing yellow (any rhythm).

Lesser channels often just posts with top marks

S Cardinal - keep south

Keep east

Lateral buoys mark deep water channel

Areas outside the main channel are often perfectly navigable by small craft. Always check chart first for hazards and available depth

W Cardinal marks west boundary of danger

Fairway buoy - safe water mark at entrance to harbour or start of buoyed channel

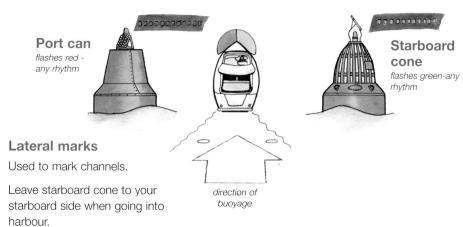

Port can
flashes red - any rhythm

Starboard cone
flashes green-any rhythm

Lateral marks

Used to mark channels.

Leave starboard cone to your starboard side when going into harbour.

direction of buoyage

IALA - B Buoyage

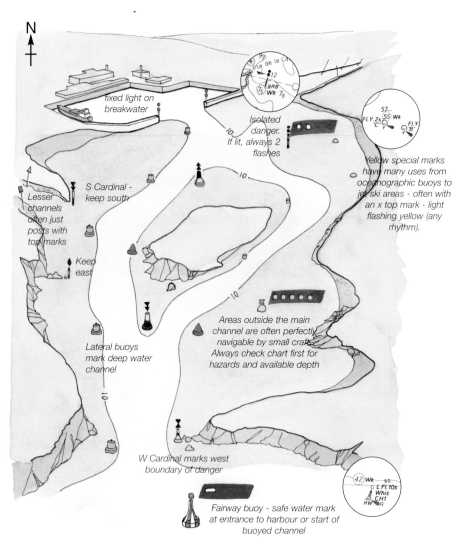

N

fixed light on breakwater

Isolated danger. If lit, always 2 flashes

S Cardinal - keep south

Lesser channels often just posts with top marks

Keep east

Yellow special marks have many uses from oceanographic buoys to jet ski areas - often with an x top mark - light flashing yellow (any rhythm).

Lateral buoys mark deep water channel

Areas outside the main channel are often perfectly navigable by small craft. Always check chart first for hazards and available depth

W Cardinal marks west boundary of danger

Fairway buoy - safe water mark at entrance to harbour or start of buoyed channel

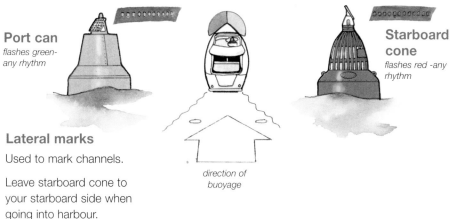

Port can
flashes green-any rhythm

Starboard cone
flashes red -any rhythm

direction of buoyage

Lateral marks

Used to mark channels.

Leave starboard cone to your starboard side when going into harbour.

Special Marks

Isolated danger mark

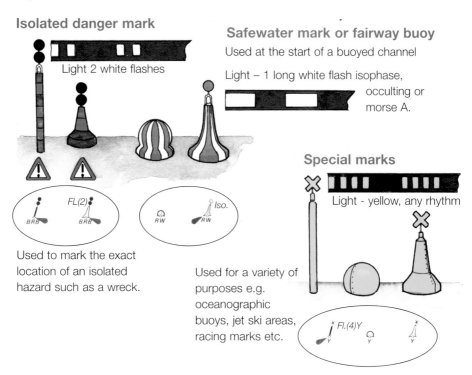

Light 2 white flashes

Safewater mark or fairway buoy

Used at the start of a buoyed channel

Light – 1 long white flash isophase, occulting or morse A.

FL(2)
BRB *BRB*

Iso.
RW *RW*

Used to mark the exact location of an isolated hazard such as a wreck.

Special marks

Light - yellow, any rhythm

Used for a variety of purposes e.g. oceanographic buoys, jet ski areas, racing marks etc.

Fl.(4)Y
Y *Y* *Y*

Traffic separation

Traffic separation schemes are denoted on a chart by purple shaded areas. Arrows on the chart denote the direction of the shipping lane.

Traffic separation schemes separate large vessels in areas of the sea prone to heavy traffic. They act as roads – all eastbound vessels on one side and westbound on another. Crossing a TSS is like crossing a road without a pedestrian crossing. Take the quickest route and make your intentions clear to the vessels using the TSS.

correct heading 90° to TSS

tide

Always point the boat at right angles to the scheme so that you show the correct aspect to oncoming traffic.

Basic ropework

Sheet bend

Useful for joining two lengths of rope together.

Cannot be untied under load.

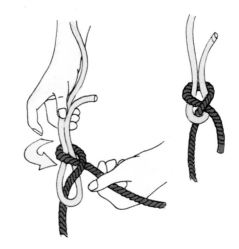

Clove Hitch

Useful for tying fenders. Easy to adjust, Use in low-load situations.

1

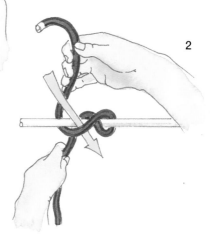

2

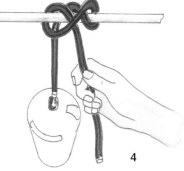

3

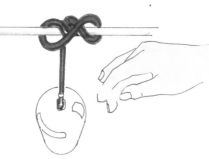

4

Bowline

Makes a loop in the end of a piece of rope. Very strong knot, ideal for mooring or permanently securing to a buoy.

Cannot be untied under load.

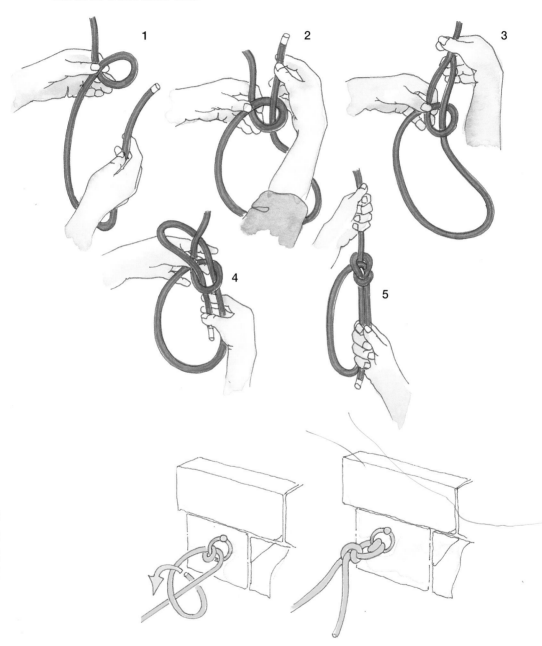

Round turn and two half hitches

Very useful for all moorings and fenders.

Can be untied under load.

Engine fault-finding

Fuel delivery

A diesel engine requires clean diesel fuel. If air enters the system, because of running out of fuel or a blockage caused by dirty fuel, the system will need to be bled. All systems differ but operate on the same principles. Consult the manual to become familiar with how your system should be bled.

The fuel run in all diesels is generally the same:

Fuel tank → Fuel shut off → Primary filter/water separator → Lift pump → Secondary or fine filter → High pressure pump → Injectors

Before bleeding a diesel engine check the following:

- Ensure tanks are filled with clean fuel.
- Check that valves and fuel shut-offs are open.
- Check for leaks in piping.
- Ensure water is drained from water separators.
- Have a good supply of fuel filters and that the filter is clean.

Lift pump can be operated manually to pump fuel from the tank to the engine.

> ## Top Tip
>
> Bleeding a diesel
> - Open bleed point.
> - Pump fuel.
> - Watch air escape.
> - When fuel comes through close bleed point.

Fine filter usually has a bleed point - undo bleed point, operate lift pump or turn over engine until a clean supply of fuel with no air bubbles is seen. Close off bleed point.

Some engines may require bleeding at the high-pressure pump and at the injectors – consult your engine manual.

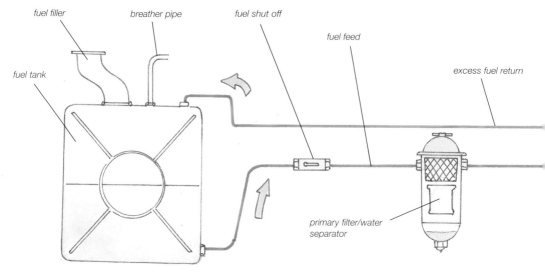

fuel filler · breather pipe · fuel shut off · fuel feed · excess fuel return · fuel tank · primary filter/water separator

Changing a flexible impellor

- Stop the engine.
- Shut off seawater intake seacock.
- Remove faceplate from raw water pump.
- Check wear on inside of faceplate – too much wear and pump forms a vacumn and does not circulate water –sometimes possible to reverse face plate if this happens.
- Slide out the impellor with pliers or an extractor, the shaft comes out too.
- Replace impellor and slide back into place.
- If vanes are missing from extracted impellor search the ports until they are found.
- Replace the face plate.
- Open seawater intake seacock.

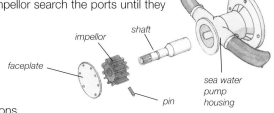

faceplate   *impellor*   *shaft*   *pin*   *sea water pump housing*

Overheating

Overheating occurs for a variety of reasons

- Blocked or partially blocked seawater inlet or strainer – check strainer.
- Insufficient water in heat exchanger or expansion tank – top up but investigate why low level.
- Worn or broken impellor in water pump – change impellor.
- Leak from water pipe – tighten clips – replace pipe – wrap pipe with self amalgamating tape.
- Thermostat faulty – check thermostat – replace or if possible remove it to get-you-home.

Top Tip

Exhaust smoke tell tales
Blue smoke = internal wear in engine.
White smoke = overheating problem.
Black smoke = fuel/air problem.

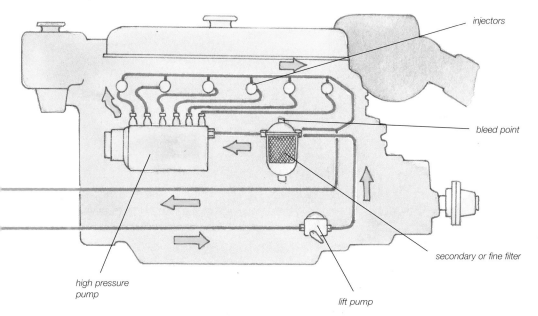

injectors

bleed point

secondary or fine filter

high pressure pump

lift pump

28 Towing

Rigging for a tow

A tow at sea puts extreme pressure on the boat's fittings to which the towline is attached. Spread the load around all of the strong points by rigging a bridle.

The tug should also rig a bridle to spread the load around the stern.

Be aware of chafe – use cloth or carpet to prevent wear from bowrollers or fairleads.

Stay clear of the stricken vessel while picking up a tow.

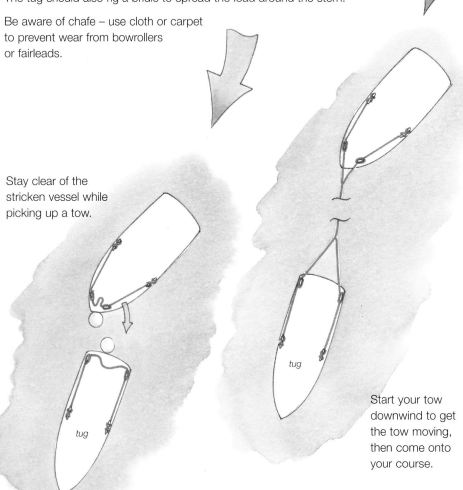

Start your tow downwind to get the tow moving, then come onto your course.

Ensure the tug stays clear of the stricken vessel when passing a line, so that stray lines do not foul the tug's prop. Be prepared to use a throwing line to pass a thicker towline, so that the vessels can stay apart. It is often wise to start the tow downwind so that momentum is built up before turning onto your course.

Towing at sea requires a long towline to reduce the snatch loads on both boats: Placing a weight along the towline helps; add to the catenary action, reducing the snatch. Anchor cable can be used as a towline – it is strong and adds weight, but will require good protection against chafe.

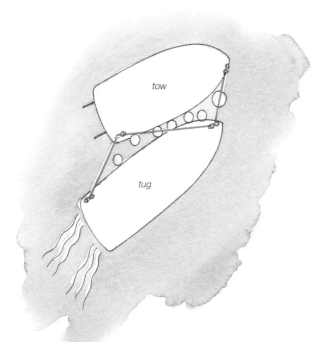

tow

tug

When going into port, tow alongside for greater manoeuvrability. Fender well and arrange the tug so that its rudder is in clear water and it is pointing slightly bows in. This helps it motor in a straight line.

If you require a tow in calm conditions with little wind, your tender may be able to get you out of trouble and tow the boat alongside, into an anchorage or up to a buoy.

Towing and the law

Arrange a fee with the tug first before any lines are taken.

Someone coming to your aid to tow, pilot, navigate or advise can be termed as a salvageable act. The amount a salver is paid is determined by the risk he takes and the life or property saved. Therefore agree a towage fee first and keep records or a log of the tow, to show you still have a say in the situation.

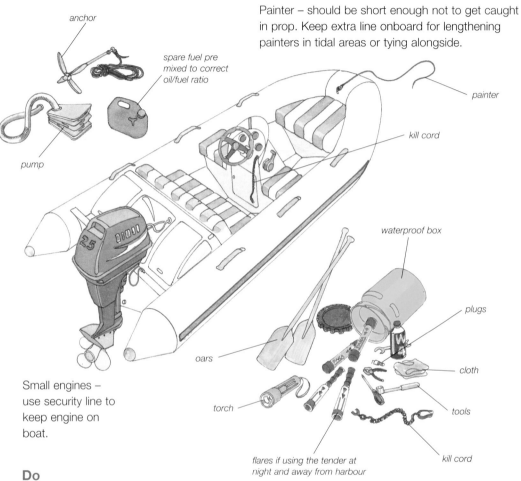

Painter – should be short enough not to get caught in prop. Keep extra line onboard for lengthening painters in tidal areas or tying alongside.

anchor

spare fuel pre mixed to correct oil/fuel ratio

painter

kill cord

pump

waterproof box

plugs

Small engines – use security line to keep engine on boat.

oars

cloth

torch

tools

flares if using the tender at night and away from harbour

kill cord

Do

- Wear lifejackets
- Load evenly
- Make extra trips as necessary
- Keep fingers clear of the sides when coming alongside
- Regularly service engine
- Use kill cord (if fitted)

Do not

- Overload
- Speed
- Drink and drive
- Load unevenly

Distress situations

Raising the alarm

Flares

- Brief the crew on how to call for help.

- The flare briefing should include: where the flares are kept; when to fire them; how they operate as all flares ignite differently.

- Ensure flares are in date and kept in a waterproof container.

- Gloves and goggles are useful to stop accidental burns.

- Fire all flares pointing slightly downwind and do not look straight at them.

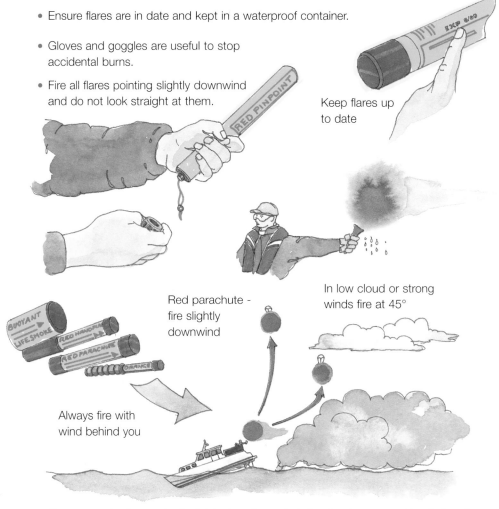

Keep flares up to date

Red parachute - fire slightly downwind

In low cloud or strong winds fire at 45°

Always fire with wind behind you

- Orange smoke for use in daylight, also gives wind direction to approaching helicopter.

- Pinpoint flares give your exact position and are ideal in low visibility or at night.

- Parachute rockets are fired downwind as they turn into the wind. Never fire if helicopter is approaching.

Other Distress signals

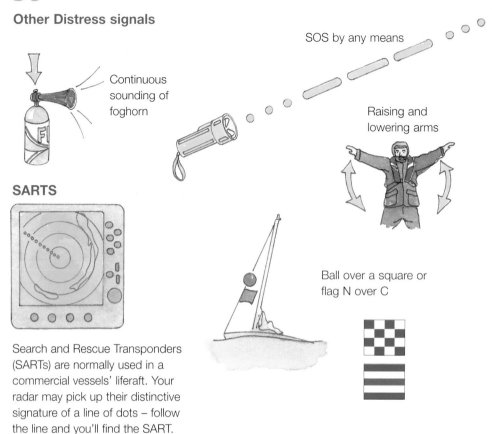

SOS by any means

Continuous
sounding of
foghorn

Raising and
lowering arms

SARTS

Ball over a square or
flag N over C

Search and Rescue Transponders
(SARTs) are normally used in a
commercial vessels' liferaft. Your
radar may pick up their distinctive
signature of a line of dots – follow
the line and you'll find the SART.

EPIRB

- Emergency Position Indicating
  Radio Beacon (EPIRB).

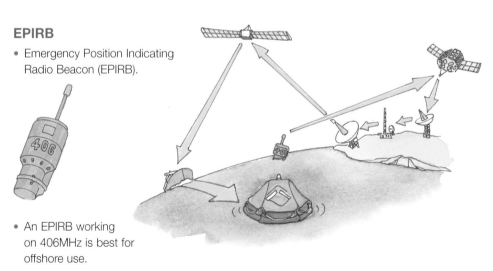

- An EPIRB working
  on 406MHz is best for
  offshore use.

- Register an EPIRB at purchase. Once activated, the EPIRB sends out an identification
  code and rough position so that the rescue centre knows what help to send and where
  to send it. EPIRBs have near Global coverage. 406 MHz EPIRBs also transmit on
  121.5MHz for homing in to your position.

- GPS EPIRB; gives your exact position to rescue services faster.

VHF

VHF voice call - select channel 16

Use VHF to alert the coastguard and other vessels in your area.

You must tell them:

- your boat's name.
- your position.
- how many people are on board.
- what assistance you require.

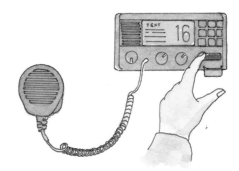

VHF is better than a mobile phone for distress calling - other vessels in your area will hear your call and the coastguard can use VHF transmissions to fix your position.

A mobile phone will only tell one person that you are in trouble; the network coverage is patchy away from land and you won't be able to talk direct to a helicopter or lifeboat.

Digital VHF (DSC) call

You may not have time to send a voice call but some modern VHF sets can:

- send a distress alert or urgency call at the press of a button.
- be linked to a GPS to send your position.

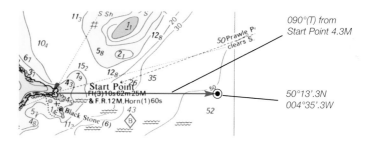

MAYDAY

When life or vessel are in grave and imminent danger

Mayday x 3

This is motor yacht Puffin x 3

Mayday yacht Puffin

(give MMSI if fitted with DSC)

My position is 50°13'.3N 04°35'.3W

We are holed and sinking and require immediate assistance

Six persons on board

Over

PAN PAN

Urgency message - if crew or vessel need assistance

Pan Pan x 3

All ships x 3

This is yacht Seaspray x 3

(give MMSI if fitted with DSC)

My position is 090°(T) from Start Point

4.3 miles

I have a broken rudder and require a tow

Four persons on board

Over

You may use a VHF radio under the supervision of a qualified person or to make a distress call - otherwise you need an operator's certificate. Contact the RYA or your National Boating Authority..

Fire control

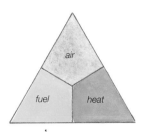

Fire Triangle

A fire needs fuel, air and heat to exist. Remove one of these elements and the fire will go out.

Prevent fires by

- Not smoking below.
- Exercising caution with cooking fats and solvents.
- Venting petrol (gasoline) vapour.
- Keeping engine bay and electrics clean.
- Installing correct size wiring.

Fire extinguishers

Extinguishers should be located near the fire they are to fight. General-purpose extinguishers are placed near entrances and escape hatches. Cabins that have only one exit point should be fitted with extinguishers and smoke alarms.

Dry powder – general purpose, but do not use on liquids.

AFFF foam – good on liquids and for general purpose.

Halocarbon/CO2 – gas for enclosed spaces, good on electrics and engines.

Fire blanket – excellent for smothering cooking fires or clothing.

Fire fighting

- Aim at base of fire.
- Smother with a blanket, ensure hands are protected.
- Splash water rather than throw.
- Smother clothing using a fire blanket.

Gas safety

- Ensure all crew know the safety routine involving gas.
- Ensure gas locker drains are clear.
- Ensure all piping is secured and protected from vibrating loose.
- Check rubber piping for brittleness.
- Shut off valve near cooker after use.
- Shut off valve in locker overnight and when left.

In the event of a leak

- Shut off gas.
- Shut off electrics.
- Open all hatches.
- Inform all aboard.
- Lift floorboards to aid ventilation because gas sinks into bilge.
- Ensure nobody smokes.
- Call a qualified engineer to test system.

Engine fire

Auto extinguishers can be combined with audible alarms so that you are aware of their operation.

- Switch off fuel.
- Switch off electrics to engine.
- Do not lift engine hatch.
- Fire the extinguishing medium through inspection hole.

If you cannot fight the fire, abandon ship.

- Consider keeping lifejackets in outside lockers so that they are available without going into the fire.
- Send Mayday.
- Use flares.
- Launch liferaft.

Taking to the liferaft

Stay with the boat – step up into a liferaft

Unless on fire, stay with the boat until the last moment. It offers the best protection, has extra supplies and is easier to spot than a liferaft. Ensure you try everything to slow the ingress of water to keep the boat afloat.

Wear lifejackets.

- Check liferaft painter is tied on.
- Launch liferaft on downwind side.
- Pull painter line to inflate.
- Stay dry – get into the liferaft from the boat.
- Fittest in first – to help others.
- Safety knife inside raft entrance to cut painter.

Cut – Stream – Close – Maintain

- Cut painter line and paddle away from danger.
- Stream the drogue.
- Close entrances to protect from waves. Ventilate raft every 30 minutes.
- Monitor casualties, bail, pump tubes, and maintain morale.
- The will to survive is your best ally.

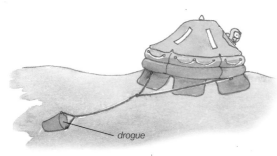

drogue

Extra supplies

Water is the single most important item to take into a liferaft.

- Food – carbohydrates are especially important.
- EPIRB.
- First aid.
- Clothing.
- Thermal protective aids.
- Hand-held VHF.
- Hand-held GPS.

Personal items such as glasses and personal medication can be pre-packed in your liferaft at a service interval or kept in a grab bag.

Helicopter rescue

The helicopter pilot will contact by VHF and give a brief on what is going to happen. The brief will include a course and speed for you to follow. Listen carefully and take notes.

It is important to steer a constant course without deviating.

A weighted line is lowered. Let it earth in the water to release static. Do not attach it to the boat. Use the line to guide the helicopter winch-man. Gloves are useful.

1 The winchman will land on deck.

2 Unhook and assess the situation.

3 The winchman takes the casualty off the boat.

4 The weighted line is used to control his swing.

Man over board (MOB)

Your actions will depend on whether you can see the casualty or not.

Initial Actions

- Shout 'Man overboard!' to alert the crew.
- Spot the MOB.
- Throw a danbuoy to give a datum.
- Press MOB 'Enter' button on the GPS.

Other actions

- Call Mayday or DSC alert.
- Prepare a lasso to throw around the MOB.
- Put a crew in harness to aid retrieval of MOB.

Note: if the MOB has no buoyancy, it may be necessary to drop them a lifering, fender or cushion to help them stay afloat before starting your approach.

Getting back - close-quarter method

Most motorboats can stop and turn around very quickly, making this method useful by day and in good visibility.

- Slow and establish wind direction.
- Turn around and drive upwind.
- Stop with the wind abeam.
- Drift downwind onto the MOB.
- Use only the engine furthest away from the MOB.

How would you recover a casualty back onboard your boat? What if they were unconscious, and what if it was the skipper? Come up with a tried and tested solution before you need it for real.

Getting back - Williamson Turn

The Williamson Turn is an initial action after a person has fallen overboard. It turns the boat back towards its wake, where the MOB should be located. It is designed for large vessels travelling at speed but works with all vessels and is a useful strategy at night.

The Williamson Turn

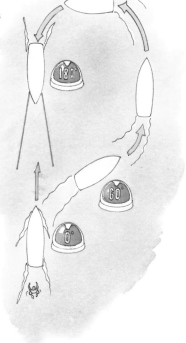

- Man overboard. Compass course noted and reciprocal course worked out. The easiest way of doing this on standard compasses is to place your hand along the compass card and read off the reciprocal heading.

- Boat steers 60 degrees to starboard. This turn to starboard opens up the turning circle to allow the boat to come back on its wake.

- Helm hard over to bring the boat to port.

- Continue with helm hard over until the boat nears its reciprocal heading, then straighten up and steer the reciprocal heading. This should bring the boat back on its wake. SLOW DOWN and look for the MOB.

- Once sighted, establish the wind direction and aim a few metres to windward of the casualty.

- Once upwind, stop and allow the wind to blow the boat onto the casualty.

Use the engine furthest away from the casualty for final positioning.

The 50-degree offset to starboard will vary as boats' turning circles differ depending on their hull configuration. Sea conditions and weather also play their part. What you are looking for is an allowance to take you back to your wake.

Treatment of cold casualty

- Change into dry clothes.
- Slowly re-warm.
- Give warm drinks.
- Plastic bags or Thermal Protective Aids help retain body heat.
- Monitor constantly and record reflexes and symptoms at 15-minute intervals.
- Get help – call for medical assistance or get them checked ashore.

31 Stability

Boats remain upright because of the relationship between their weight (centre of gravity) and buoyancy.

A boat's weight represents gravity pushing downwards into the water. The centre of the weight (hull, engine, superstructure) is called the Centre of Gravity, or CG.

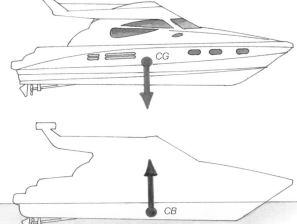

The upward force of buoyancy stops the boat from sinking. Buoyancy depends on the amount of water the boat displaces, and this in turn depends on the size and shape of the hull in the water. The centre of the buoyancy is called CB.

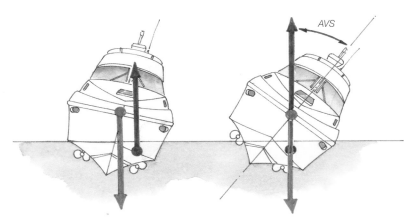

If the CB moves to one side faster than the CG, the boat is stable.

Once the CG rolls over the CB, the boat will roll over. This point is called its Angle of Vanishing Stability (AVS).

The critical point on a motorboat is at 35-40 degrees, when the air intakes on the side start to scoop water and flood. This angle of listing can be caused by large seas on the beam, broaching or by overcrowding one side of the boat.

Reduction in stability

Placing a flybridge on a boat not designed for one will significantly affect its stability as it raises the CG on the boat. Arches, radar and top weight all contribute to a reduction in stability.

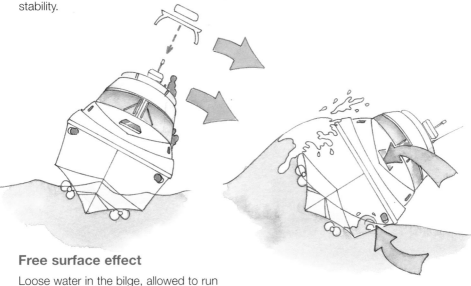

Free surface effect

Loose water in the bilge, allowed to run freely from one side to the other as the boat moves, greatly effects stability by moving the CG.

Watch out for and prevent

- Extra top weight.
- Knockdown by breaking seas.
- Broaching.
- Water flooding through hatches or air inlets.
- Overloading or bad trim.

So...

- Close hatches before going to sea
- Read the forecast
- Ensure cockpit area drains quickly and that drains are not blocked
- Make sure engine air inlet is as high as is practicable
- Ensure bilge pumps work
- Avoid rough areas, such as tide races and overfalls

More information is available in RYA Book, *Stability and Buoyancy*.

Worldwide all vessels need to comply with these regulations.

The exact wording of the regulations is used with some explanatory notes provided by the RYA.

Radar reflector - *Regulation 19.2.1.7.*

All ships shall have, if less than 150 gross registered tonnes and if practicable, a radar reflector or other means, to enable detection by ships navigating by radar at both 9 and 3 GHz.

RYA Note: 'When practicable' means that if you can carry a radar reflector, you should. Both passive radar reflectors and active devices are available.

Lifesaving signals - *Regulation 29.*

An illustrated table describing the life-saving signals shall be readily available to the officer of the watch on every ship to which this chapter applies. The signals shall be used by ships or persons in distress when communicating with life-saving stations, maritime rescue units and aircraft engaged in SAR ops.

RYA Note: Keeping this table on board will mean that you comply with this regulation - the table can be found on pages 120/121

Danger messages - *Regulation 31.*

Masters are to communicate information on navigational dangers. These include, for example, a dangerous derelict or other dangerous obstructions, tropical storms, winds of Force 10 or more for which no warning has been received. The form that information is sent is not obligatory and it can be transmitted in plain language or using the International Code of Signals. Contracting governments must promulgate any danger information received and messages must be free of charge to ships.

RYA Note: This regulation basically means that you, as skipper, have a responsibility to pass on information about navigation dangers to the Coastguard by any means that you can.

Danger messages - *Regulation 32.*

This regulation deals with the kind of information required in danger messages. It also has examples of typical danger messages.

RYA Note: This regulation means that you should pass on sufficient information about any navigation dangers you experience or witness (For example: position, nature of danger, time seen/witnessed, any other useful information) to enable other shipping in the area to avoid it.

Distress messages - *obligations and procedures - Regulation 33.*

Masters are obliged to respond to distress messages from any source. Ships can be requisitioned by the master of a ship in distress or the Search and Rescue (SAR) authorities.

RYA Note: This regulation reinforces the duty of skippers to respond to any distress messages they hear.

Safe navigation and avoidance of dangerous situations -
Regulation 34.

Voyage planning is required on all vessels that go to sea. "Going to sea is defined as proceeding outside of categorized waters". You can get more information about what constitutes categorised waters from the MCA and the RYA.

MCA guidance notes say for 'small craft and pleasure vessels, the degree of voyage planning will be dependent on the size of vessel, its crew and the length of the voyage'. The MCA says that it 'expects all mariners to make a careful assessment of any proposed voyage taking into account all dangers to navigation, weather forecasts, tidal predictions and other relevant factors including the competence of the crew.'

RYA Note: Skippers should note that this regulation changes the status of passage planning on small boats from simply good practice to a requirement under UK law. No formal written plan is required and there is no set format. Anyone who goes on an RYA practical course will be confident of their ability to plan a cruise competently. Anyone who is not confident of their passage planning ability should take a suitable RYA practical course. (see inside back cover for more details).

Misuse of distress signals -
Regulation 35.

"Distress signals only to be used for the proper purpose".

RYA Note: This regulation reinforces the fact that distress signals have a life saving role and should not be misused.

Life saving signals

To be used by Ships, Aircraft or Persons in Distress

Maritime and Coastguard Agency

Search and Rescue Unit Replies

You have been seen, assistance will be given as soon as possible.

OR

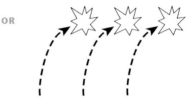

Orange smoke flare.

Three white star signals or three light and sound rockets fired at approximately 1 minute intervals.

Surface to Air Signals

Note: Use International Code of Signal by means of lights or flags or by laying out the symbol on the deck or ground with items which have a high contrast to the background.

Message	International Code of Signals		ICAO Visual Signals
I require assistance	V ✕	···▬	V
I require medical assistance	W ▣	▪▬▪▪	X
No or negative	N ▨	▬▪	N
Yes or affirmative	C ≡	▬▪▬▪	Y
Proceeding in this direction			↑

Air to Surface Direction Signals

Sequence of 3 manoeuvres meaning proceed to this direction.

1

Circle vessel at least once.

2

Cross low, ahead a vessel rocking wings.

3

Overfly vessel and head in required direction.

Your assistance is no longer required.

Cross low, astern of vessel rocking wings.

Note: As a non preferred alternative to rocking wings, varying engine tone or volume may be used.

Shore to Ship Signals

Safe to land here.

OR

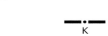
K

Vertical waving of both arms, white flag, light or flare.　　Morse code signal by light or sound.

Landing here is dangerous. Additional signals mean safer landing in direction indicated.

OR

S: •••
Morse code signals by light or sound.
R: •—•
Land to the right of your current heading.
L: •—••
Land to the left of your current heading.

Horizontal waving of white flag, light or flare. Putting one flag, light or flare on ground and moving off with a second indicates direction of safer landing.

Air to Surface Replies

Message Understood.

　OR　　OR　　OR
— T　OR　•—• R

Drop a message.　　Rocking wings.　　Flashing landing or navigation lights on and off twice.　　Morse code signal by light.

Message Not Understood – Repeat.

OR　OR

•—• R　•—•—• P　— T

Straight and level flight.　　Circling.　　Morse code signal by light.

Surface to Air Replies

Message Understood – I will comply.

OR OR
— T

Change course to required direction.　　Morse code signal by light.　　Code & answering pendant "Close Up".

I am unable to comply.

OR
—•
N

Note: Use the signal most appropriate to prevailling conditions,

Morse code signal by light.　　International flag "N".

123

RYA *Membership*

Promoting and Protecting Boating
www.rya.org.uk

RYA Membership

Promoting and Protecting Boating

The RYA is the national organisation which represents the interests of everyone who goes boating for pleasure.

The greater the membership, the louder our voice when it comes to protecting members' interests.

Apply for membership today, and support the RYA, to help the RYA support you.

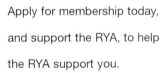

Benefits of Membership

- Access to expert advice on all aspects of boating from legal wrangles to training matters
- Special members' discounts on a range of products and services including boat insurance, books, videos and class certificates
- Free issue of certificates of competence, increasingly asked for by everyone from overseas governments to holiday companies, insurance underwriters to boat hirers

- Access to the wide range of RYA publications, including the quarterly magazine
- Third Party insurance for windsurfing members
- Free Internet access with RYA-Online
- Special discounts on AA membership
- Regular offers in RYA Magazine
- ...and much more

Join now - membership form opposite

Join online at www.rya.org.uk

Visit our website for information, advice, members' services and web shop.

Join the RYA now!

1 Important To help us comply with Data Protection legislation, please tick *either* Box A or Box B (you must tick Box A to ensure you receive the full benefits of RYA membership). The RYA will not pass your data to third parties.

☐ **A.** I wish to join the RYA and receive future information on member services, benefits (as listed in RYA Magazine and website) and offers.

☐ **B.** I wish to join the RYA but do not wish to receive future information on member services, benefits (as listed in RYA Magazine and website) and offers.

When completed, please send this form to: RYA, RYA House, Ensign Way, Hamble, Southampton, SO31 4YA

2 Title | Forename | Surname | Date of Birth (D D / M M / Y Y) | Male | Female

1.
2.
3.
4.

Address

Town | **County** | **Post Code**

Evening Telephone | **Daytime Telephone**

email

Signature: _____ **Date:** _____

3 Type of membership required: *(Tick Box)*

☐ **Personal** *Current full annual rate £33 or £30 by Direct Debit*

☐ **Under 21** *Current full annual rate £11 (no reduction for Direct Debit)*

☐ **Family*** *Current full annual rate £50 or £47 by Direct Debit*

* *Family Membership: 2 adults plus any under 21s all living at the same address*

4 Please tick ONE box to show your main boating interest.

☐ Yacht Racing   ☐ Yacht Cruising
☐ Dinghy Racing   ☐ Dinghy Cruising
☐ Personal Watercraft ☐ Inland Waterways
☐ Powerboat Racing   ☐ Windsurfing
☐ Motor Boating   ☐ Sportsboats and RIBs

Please see Direct Debit form overleaf

RYA

Instructions to your Bank or Building Society to pay by Direct Debit

Please complete this form and return it to:
Royal Yachting Association, RYA House, Ensign Way, Hamble, Southampton, Hampshire SO31 4YA

DIRECT Debit

To The Manager: _____ Bank/Building Society

Address: _____

Post Code: _____

2. Name(s) of account holder(s)

_____

3. Branch Sort Code

	—		—	

4. Bank or Building Society account number

Banks and Building Societies may not accept Direct Debit instructions for some types of account

Cash, Cheque, Postal Order enclosed £ _____
Made payable to the Royal Yachting Association

077 **Office use only:** Membership Number Allocated _____

Originators Identification Number

9	5	5	2	1	3

5. RYA Membership Number (For office use only)

_____

6. Instruction to pay your Bank or Building Society

Please pay Royal Yachting Association Direct Debits from the account detailed in this instruction subject to the safeguards assured by The Direct Debit Guarantee.
I understand that this instruction may remain with the Royal Yachting Association and, if so, details will be passed electronically to my Bank/Building Society.

Signature(s) _____

Date _____

Office use / Centre Stamp